"For over 20 years, our business has been to drive leads to many of the industries that sell to homeowners. The missing piece, in many cases, has been the lack of training on how to take those leads and convert them into customers. This book demonstrates a proven process to increase sales and revenue for those businesses and sales professionals. "

—**Todd Baldwin,** CEO,
Everyday Media LLC

"This book uses practical applications and Sandler sales language to teach us how to interact with prospective clients, how to find out what is important to them, and how to move them to act, especially when meeting in their own home. This is a special presentation to which every financial/insurance representative should be exposed."

—**David Bostick,** General Manager,
Texas Agency, National Life Group

SELLING TO HOMEOWNERS
The Sandler Way

SELLING TO HOMEOWNERS

The Sandler Way

A Proven Process for Selling Products and Services to Consumers in Their Home

KIM BOOKER & CHIP DOYLE

Sandler Training

© 2015 Sandler Systems, Inc. All rights reserved.

Reproduction, modification, storage in a retrieval system or retransmission, in any form or by any means, electronic, mechanical or otherwise, is strictly prohibited without the prior written permission of Sandler Systems, Inc.

S Sandler Training (with design), Sandler, Sandler Selling System, Sandler Submarine (words and design) and Sandler Pain Funnel are registered service marks of Sandler Systems, Inc.

"Extended DISC" and "Extended DISC Diamond" are registered trademarks of Extended DISC International Oy, Ltd. Used with permission.

Because the English language lacks a generic singular pronoun that indicates both genders, we have used the masculine pronouns for the sake of style, readability, and brevity. This material applies to both men and women.

Paperback: 978-0-692-54742-7
E-book: 978-0-692-54903-2

Acknowledgments

Many thanks to our loving spouses Scott and Debra, family and friends for their support. And sincere gratitude to the entire Sandler network for perpetuating the Sandler concepts.

We both would also like to recognize our valued clients that have taught us so much about the varied industries in this book. It's one thing to write about or teach a concept. It's quite another to use these skills and get outside one's comfort zone. This book would not have been possible without the hundreds of companies and thousands of salespeople who have used these skills and helped us refine them over many years.

CONTENTS

Foreword... ix

Introduction: *Why Should You Do Something Different?* xi

Chapter One: *Why Customers Buy*.......................... 1

Chapter Two: *Voice-to-Voice—First Impressions Matter*..... 23

Chapter Three: *Set the Stage for Success* 41

Chapter Four: *Could Asking Questions Be the Answer?* 63

Chapter Five: *Are They Willing and Able?*.................. 89

Chapter Six: *When in the Customer's House,
Let the Customer Buy* 113

Chapter Seven: *Don't Go Broke Being Busy*............... 127

Chapter Eight: *Putting It All Together*..................... 147

FOREWORD

Kim Booker and Chip Doyle bring a wealth of experience to the complex subject of selling effectively to homeowners and a pragmatic, real-world approach that has delivered positive results in both the short and long term to sellers in a wide variety of industries. It's a pleasure to be part of their project and to introduce you to this book.

When I first heard their idea for a book introducing the Sandler Selling System® methodology to salespeople whose prospects are homeowners, I was excited for three reasons. First, I knew they each had an impressive record of successfully training such sales teams—on opposite sides of the country, no less!—and I knew that each would include important personal experiences. Second, I had a feeling that their perspectives would complement each other well in a project of this kind. And third, I looked forward to their using this material to disprove a common myth about the Sandler® principles: namely, that they are primarily or exclusively relevant only to business-to-business sales models.

As *Selling to Homeowners the Sandler Way* proves in every chapter, the concepts and strategies our company's founder David Sandler laid out are relevant—and career-changing—for any open-minded salesperson tasked with selling anything to anyone. All that's required is a willingness to change your behaviors, your attitude and your technique and a desire to commit to a real-world learning process that's based on ongoing reinforcement and continuous improvement over time.

Success is our mission, our promise and our brand. It's the goal of our clients—current and future, global and local—on the street corner and in the boardroom. With this book, Kim Booker and Chip Doyle remind us that it's also the goal of our sales clients who connect with prospects in the living room and over the kitchen table. If you're one of those clients, I think you'll find what follows to be an invaluable refresher. If you sell to homeowners and you haven't yet worked with Sandler, we look forward to continuing the discussion with you.

David H. Mattson
President/CEO, Sandler Training

INTRODUCTION

Why Should You Do Something Different?

Why should you do something different?

Maybe you shouldn't.

Maybe your sales results are steady or even spectacular. Maybe the methods getting you leads and referrals are working well. Maybe your company's closing percentages are high because of a strong sales process. Maybe your competition is far behind, and you don't feel the pressure to discount to close more business.

Maybe you are happy with the money you are making, the type of customers you are serving, and the time and resources needed to acquire and keep those customers. Great! If so, you may not be looking for ways to improve.

However—if you are like most sales professionals and business owners who sell primarily to customers in their homes—you may be tired of doing the same things over and over again and getting the same (disappointing) results.

You may have a challenge in one or more of the areas we identified above. Or, things might be going pretty well and your business is good, but you know there is an opportunity to increase your sales and get a larger share of the potential market. You are looking for ways to improve and become even more effective. In that case, this book *is* for you.

Some of the most common problems we at Sandler hear from professionals selling to customers in their homes are:

- Frustration with overall sales results.
- Concern about the length of sales cycles and the number of people who say, "I'll think it over."
- Difficulty dealing with multiple decision makers who have different expectations and decision-making styles—and who may not even be home at the same time.
- Pressure from prospects for salespeople to send email quotes and "follow up"—a process that results in playing voicemail tag or leaving perpetually unreturned calls and emails.
- Pressure to discount in order to get business, resulting in reduced margins.
- No good way to identify from a sales call who is most likely to buy and why.
- Being increasingly "busy" with calls, quotes, follow up, etc., but not closing enough business.
- Frustration with hours spent on proposals to homeowners who don't buy from anyone, not even the competition.
- Disappointment when sales that should close on the first call, do not and having no time for follow up.

- And, if you're management: No consistent hiring or training process; some salespeople "get it" and some don't, with no real way to predict accurately who will be successful.

If any of those problems resonate with you or your team, you might want to keep reading.

IN-HOME SELLING IS DIFFERENT

If you or anyone in your company go into the home for any part of the sales process, this book is for you. The techniques we will be sharing apply especially to professionals offering products or services to customers in their homes. This kind of selling is different from selling business-to-business.

In the unique world of in-home selling, you are not calling on a business where, since the decision makers are at work, they are expected to make business and financial decisions. You are entering your customers' personal and private space, where decision making can be a bit more fluid.

Different rules apply in the home. Children and pets may reign supreme. All decision makers may not be there from 9–5, Monday through Friday. Often homeowners have never before purchased your product or service. Or, if they have, they probably had a bad experience. (Otherwise, why would they be calling you?) In-home selling unfolds in an environment that can easily become an obstacle for the untrained sales professional.

Have you ever had any of these things happen to you on a sales call?

"Jim, please excuse Spot. He doesn't bite most people. He may growl occasionally. Just ignore him while we walk through the house."

"My husband was planning to be here, but he got called in early. He said just leave your quote on the counter. He has a couple more people coming by tomorrow. I have to run out in 15 minutes—will it take longer than that?"

"Wow, I never knew plants and shrubs could cost that much. If we decide to do this, it will cut into our family vacation. We will have to think about it and get back to you."

Let's be honest. Because you sell in this arena, you face a lot of unusual situations. You deal with personal space, personal relationships and personal financial decisions. The good news, however, is this:

You have been invited into their home.

Most homeowners are too busy to shop around if they have no intention of buying. If you follow the right process, you have a much better chance of closing the sale than you would if you were calling on a business customer.

You have an even stronger advantage when you learn the right process, set yourself apart and allow the customer to buy. Our objective in this book is to help you reach your goals by giving you the tools you need to become more effective.

WHY *SELLING TO HOMEOWNERS THE SANDLER WAY* IS DIFFERENT

For more than four decades, Sandler has trained tens of thousands of sales professionals, managers and business owners in industries that sell to customers in their homes. Sandler trainers—the two authors included—have gone on sales and service calls. We understand this unique selling environment.

Why Should You Do Something Different?   xv

In this book, we will introduce you to a complete sales process that is proven to succeed for in-home sales professionals. We will also provide you with resource options to develop over time, since reinforcement and practice are keys to success with in-home selling.

The strategies and techniques you will find here work across multiple industries, including yours. This book can help you whether you are experienced or a rookie, whether your title has the word "sales" in it or not. If you keep an open mind and commit to practicing what we share with you, you can see strong improvement over time.

We are emphasizing keeping an open mind and being willing to practice for a reason. Salespeople most frequently fail to see better results because they fail to do things differently. You didn't get your current sales habits overnight, and you won't change without time and energy. If you are willing to make some changes, though, we can show you a process that will improve your sales results.

This book is designed for those who sell directly to consumers in their homes, including, but not limited to, these industries:

- Custom-home building
- Fencing and gates
- Financial planning
- Floor covering
- Garage door installation and repair
- Home repair
- HVAC
- Insurance
- Interior design
- Landscaping
- Medical caregiving

- Movers
- Multi-level marketing (home-based business opportunities)
- Outdoor living
- Painters
- Pest control
- Plumbing
- Real estate
- Remodeling
- Roofing
- Security systems
- Siding and insulation
- Solar panels
- Swimming pool construction/maintenance
- Window installation

Are you ready for better sales?

Great! Let's start with a deeper understanding of why people buy and the purchasing "system" that most of your potential customers have learned.

CHAPTER ONE

Why Customers Buy

Mike, a floor-covering professional, shows up right on time for his appointment in Mrs. Doyle's home. He makes small talk about the nice weather and the sweet little dog who is now licking the brand-new samples he brought with him. He recalls that he is supposed to transition to the sales part of the call.

"Tell me, where is the wood flooring you are looking to replace?" he asks.

That's the only question Mike asks during this meeting.

The homeowner shows Mike the area in the living room. Mike measures while Mrs. Doyle looks through samples. She says she wants to replace the flooring and will probably get other bids and look around a little bit before buying. Mike nods and says he talks to a lot of homeowners who say that. What she doesn't tell Mike is that she and her husband plan to put the house on the market in four weeks and either rent it out or sell it.

Blissfully ignorant, Mike says, "You know, we have some great specials going on right now. No one can beat our price when you figure in the great service we provide."

Mike proceeds to caution the homeowner about looking at other vendors. Most of them, he warns, have bad and unreliable installation crews; they may try to sell a lower-quality product that won't last as long as the materials his company uses; they haven't been in business as long as his company has; and so on. She thanks him for the advice. They head to the kitchen table.

Mike decides that, since she says she is looking at other vendors, he had best give her three flooring options in case another company offers a lower-quality product.

"We call them good, better and best," he says, showing off the samples. He presents various packages and pricing structures. Then he explains, at some length, how many years the company has been in business. The homeowner keeps nodding obediently.

Mike pulls out his tablet computer and pulls up a presentation. The presentation explains how flooring is installed, the various differences in materials and other important points.

The homeowner asks Mike to send her an email explaining all the options so she can review everything with her husband. She tells Mike she appreciates all the options he has provided for her and how knowledgeable he is about flooring materials. She says they are just starting to look around and they will get back to him.

MIKE IS OPTIMISTIC

Mike feels pretty good about his visit. He gave it his best shot. The customer was friendly, and Mike gave her a lot of information about why she should buy from him over any competitor.

At the end of a day of calls like this, Mike spends about two hours emailing quotes to people who have requested them. He attaches these quotes with care, after double-checking each one; each has all the relevant part numbers and, of course, each has all the options he promised each person. He sends each of these emails with the same subject line: "Floor quote." The text of each message also is the same for each person. It reads: "It was great to meet with you today. Here is the quote for the new flooring. Let me know if you have any more questions. You can reach me at [phone number]."

The next day, Mike is busy with new calls, but none of them close on the spot. Mike's manager says he is not closing more sales because he doesn't follow up enough. It's hard to find the time, with all the people he has quoted. He leaves many messages, but if the prospects call back at all, it is while he is on another appointment.

He has so many prospects and so many new appointments, he is unsure how to prioritize. He does call Mrs. Doyle a couple of times, but he only gets voicemail and never a call back. He is disappointed because he thought she would talk to her husband and at least let him know if they received any other bids.

Wait a minute. What do you think? Did she tell Mike she would get back to him that week? Did she say anything directly about buying from him?

Nope!

She was being polite. Politeness can sound like an agreement to buy, but it wasn't ever what Mrs. Doyle came out and said.

Did she buy from another company the very same week, in order to get her property ready for sale?

Why, yes, she did!

WHO CONTROLS MOST SALES CALLS? PROSPECTS!

Prospects have a system, but most salespeople do not.

When we ask business owners, managers and sales professionals, "What is your current selling system/process?" we usually get answers like this:

"I go off what the customer says and take it from there."

"I compliment their home, ask a couple of questions and look at their current unit. Then I go over our brochure and talk about whatever product I recommend. They usually want me to email the quote, and they always have to talk it over as a couple. I either call them or they call me a few days later."

"I have been doing this job for quite a while. I can ask just a couple of questions and quickly figure out what product they are likely to need. I have all my brochures ready, and I write the estimate right then and there. I am usually in and out in less than half an hour. If they don't buy right then, I am too busy to follow up, so I tell them to call me if they are interested. Then, I move on to the next one."

These answers may sound familiar to you. You may even find yourself asking, "What's the problem?"

When you look at how often the opportunities in question

close, however, the closing ratios tend to be significantly lower than what business owners and salespeople want.

Remember: These prospects have let you into their home. They have taken the time and effort to prepare for a face-to-face meeting with you. You are right where the decisions are made. Unlike corporate selling, where there can be many decision makers in many locations with lots going on behind the scenes, you have a big advantage. You have reached the inner sanctum. You should be closing at an aggressive rate, a rate that makes both you and your manager happy.

Yet without a consistent selling system, your sales calls may be similar to Mike's.

Who was in charge of that exchange?

Mrs. Doyle.

Who gave her that control?

Mike!

THE BUYER-SELLER DANCE

This brings us to what we call the "Buyer-Seller Dance." Only one person leads that dance. It's either the salesperson or the prospect. It's never both.

It may come as a surprise, but your prospects use a buying system. So do you, each time you encounter a salesperson you know wants to sell you something.

You have played the buyer's role many times. When you encounter a salesperson like Mike, you employ some basic tools in order to protect yourself. You've had years of experience in using these tools, though you might not always be able to identify what they are in words. Mrs. Doyle might not have been able to describe exactly what she was doing to protect herself. But she was in control of the process from beginning to end.

In fact, Mike's starting point should have been to have some sympathy for these protective strategies that buyers use. Buyers have been burned by salespeople so often in the past that they develop a kind of radar for people who make false promises and set unrealistic expectations. Getting angry or frustrated with buyers for using these systems will not help you close deals.

> **SANDLER RULE**
>
> *There are no bad prospects—only bad salespeople.*

You can learn how to deal with the most predictable buyer behaviors by deciding ahead of time what you will do in response. The buying systems explained below apply to both prospects and buyers (customers). (By the way, we refer to everyone as a prospect until the person actually buys something.)

> *Your job is to figure out which prospects will buy and which will not. In order to do that, you must understand the buyer's system!*

THE FIRST STEP OF THE BUYER'S SYSTEM: MISLEADING

Unfortunately, homeowners don't always play straight with salespeople. They may tell you half the truth or they may "accidentally" omit important details, as Mrs. Doyle did. Then again, they may lie to you outright. (Hard to believe, we know, but apparently it does happen.)

Here are some of the most common ways buyers mislead:

- "We always get three bids."

    Prospect translation: "If I say this, the salesperson surely will give me the best price and won't pressure me to buy now. The truth is, I don't have time to get any other bids."

- "We're just looking."

    Prospect translation: "We need it installed by the end of the month but I don't want any pressure to buy."

- "I make all the decisions on home repairs."

    Prospect translation: "My spouse will need to weigh in on this, but I don't want the salesperson to finagle some way to get us to meet at the same time."

- "I will have to run this by my spouse."

    Prospect translation: "My spouse doesn't care what I buy, but I'm saying that so that if I decide not to buy, I have that as an excuse."

- "We are basing our decision solely on price."

    Prospect translation: "We buy lots of things because of convenience, value and service—or because we do not have time to invite three companies into our home."

You get the picture. That's the world you live in as a sales professional. That may sound harsh, until you realize that you yourself have done this for most of your adult life at one time or another. Haven't you ever gotten a phone solicitation where you told the salesperson you were "not interested" before you even knew what the call was about? That's the real world. Saying that doesn't make you a bad person. It makes you a prospect.

Prospects are especially guarded at the beginning of the sales process. If you've ever seen a prospect walk into a kitchen-and-bath showroom, you know it's quite common for the prospect to say, "We're just looking." You probably also know that homeowners don't generally take time off from work on a Tuesday afternoon to look at kitchen and bath fixtures to pass the time.

Similarly, the homeowner calling to get a quote for lawn maintenance who says, "We're happy with our landscaper," probably isn't entirely happy. Along the same lines, the homeowner who says, "We will go with the lowest price," probably doesn't have time to secure multiple quotes. You've met these folks. We all have.

On the other hand, not everything homeowners say is meant to mislead. The challenge for salespeople is to know the difference. It would be a lot easier to avoid being manipulated if you knew someone was going to lie to you all the time, about everything. Instead, you have to remain constantly aware that information from prospects may or may not be valid.

The misinformation prospects give you is a little like salt on a salad: they sprinkle in just enough to change the flavor and make it taste better to them. Don't be surprised when they do that. You would do it, too, in their place.

It's your job to develop a detective's ability to sense when people are telling the truth and when they are distorting or omitting information.

You might ask, "But why do they mislead me?" There is no one reason why prospects mislead or lie to salespeople. Rather, it's a lot of little reasons.

Sometimes prospects mislead you to be polite. Suppose a friend's home had new furniture that you thought was gaudy and unattractive. If your friend asked you if you like his new furniture, how would you respond? It would take a very close friend to answer that question truthfully. Even a close friend might not tell the whole truth. The same applies to prospects. You may ask people whether they are interested in your product or service, and they cordially agree they are in order to remain polite. (There are a lot of polite people out there.)

Sometimes prospects mislead you because they have had a bad experience before. Even though we here at Sandler work mostly with sales professionals, most of their business cards do not even have the word "sales" in their titles. Why don't they? Sales is the most vital position for a company's success. There is a saying: "Nothing happens until a sale is made." So, why aren't people jumping out of their seats to volunteer that they work in sales? You know why. Some of the tactics used by salespeople over the years have given this great profession a (mostly) unfounded, tarnished reputation. Your prospects don't want to get manipulated by "another salesperson like the one who burned me last time." Neither would you!

Sometimes prospects mislead you because they think that if they don't, they will be maneuvered into something they don't want to do. Have you ever known those self-described "great negotiators" who repeat the phrase, "That's too high!" even though it might be the most rock-bottom price they've ever seen? Somebody taught them that trick as a way of keeping salespeople off balance. Unfortunately, many sales professionals buy right into this. Their response is, "OK, where do I need to be?" They begin discounting, even though price was never the issue. Many salespeople habitually play the submissive role because they've convinced themselves it will get them closer to a sale. But you don't have to play that role.

At the end of the day, it doesn't matter why you can't assume prospects are always telling you the truth. What matters is that you lose a lot of time and waste a lot of energy when you do.

THE SECOND STEP IN THE BUYER'S SYSTEM: GET INFORMATION

Then there are the prospects who happily solicit your ideas, your solution for fixing their problems and your pricing. Next thing you know, they pull one of these:

a. Turn the job into a "do it yourself" project.
b. Subcontract the job out to someone who is "kind of" in the same industry.
c. Use your work to give a head start to a competitor who did not offer the same comprehensive solution you did, but who ended up doing "kind of" the same thing you wanted to do at a lower price.

This is another reality of today's world. Buyers have learned it's easy to get salespeople to give them everything they need.

Many salespeople are taught that being asked for proposals, options and all the details (meaning part numbers, detailed pricing, step-by-step instructions and so on) are all "buying signals."

Wrong!

Prospects like getting information because information is valuable. Lots of salespeople think their job is to do whatever it takes to make prospects happy. Without any commitment, however, you can easily become the dreaded "unpaid consultant."

An unpaid consultant is the knowledgeable, likeable professional who assesses a situation, tells prospects about a better way of doing something, then offers lots of information without getting any kind of commitment or a clear next step. Even better (from the prospect's point of view), many unpaid consultants will send all of that information, free, via email so it can easily be forwarded to a competitor.

Again—sound familiar?

THE THIRD STEP IN THE BUYER'S SYSTEM: BE POLITE, AND MAKE NO COMMITMENTS

If, in fact, the salesperson has something of value, the prospect will often want to keep future communication open—without committing to anything. Here's what this typically sounds like:

"Send me some literature."

"This looks interesting."

"Can you call me back in about three weeks?"

Prospects know that the best way to get a salesperson to go away without pressing for a decision is to act interested and positive about some future sale. They know that if they act interested, they have leverage to go back to step two for more information, lower prices, extra features, and so on. Then they can share this information with other salespeople—the ones who wind up getting their business.

This can also happen if prospects are not interested at all. Keeping options open eliminates any "objection handling" they know the salesperson will employ and avoids any dreaded "closing techniques." Prospects may compliment you on your presentation; your knowledge; your greater professionalism compared to the other guys; and on and on. They know most salespeople may call once to follow up, but they can dodge that call to avoid having to deal with you again.

You leave with no clear next step in place, and you may even promise to continue to provide more information. Why? Because you heard some positive comments. As a result, you now have a little stash of "hopium," the drug of choice for too many sales professionals.

Get real! You have no reason to believe this prospect will buy. Yet, because the interaction seemed so positive, you go away, like Mike did, with a great feeling: "This one's gonna close."

Sounds familiar, doesn't it?

THE LAST STEP IN THE BUYER'S SYSTEM: GO INTO HIDING

After misleading you, getting lots of information and keeping their options open by making no commitment, seemingly imminent purchasers of whatever it is you are selling have a strange habit of disappearing.

They don't return your phone calls or emails. They may have no further interest in your product or service, they may have chosen one of your competitors or they may still be in evaluation mode, entertaining other quotes, estimates or bids. One of our clients names this the "Prospect Protection Program." It's as though the Justice Department has swept in and given prospects a new identity. They are gone without a trace—until you drive by and find a competitor's truck in front of their house doing the work that should have gone to you.

Some prospects do put two or three salespeople through the wringer—getting each to spend hours of time driving, presenting and estimating—before deciding to "do nothing for now."

But don't worry. This book will help you to identify who is most likely to buy so you can become more professional and effective at quickly deciding who the best prospects are as well as who is *not* a good fit for your product/service.

WHICH PROSPECTS EVENTUALLY BUY?

Customers purchase for any number of reasons: pleasure, ego, status, security, belonging, safety, retaliation, betrayal, frustration, privacy and avoiding embarrassment, to name a few. Most of these motivators are related somehow to Pain (one of the steps of the Sandler Selling System).

> **SANDLER RULE**
> People buy emotionally, then justify
> their decisions intellectually.

Even social pressure to match the neighbor's pool, win "yard of the month" or any of a hundred other reasons can be powerful motivators. These motivators may sound at first like pleasure, but they arise out of some level of discomfort. (Example: "If I don't have an outdoor kitchen, my in-laws will never stop bugging me about how our house is not as nice as theirs.")

Psychologists know, and you should too, that all human behavior, including buying behavior, is driven by emotion. Any situation where someone buys—or doesn't buy—is related to that person's personal emotional condition. A brand-new air conditioner may be coveted by some people in the same town where others are happy to sit on a shady porch on hot days. Some homeowners will spend enormous amounts of money on kitchens and bathroom upgrades, while others are perfectly content with long-time appliances and amenities. Some people want a very basic pool while others want an elaborate backyard oasis. It's the emotion that drives the decision to buy—or not.

Bottom line: Customers buy to eliminate problems that cause them pain.

This pain, by definition, is a problem that someone wants solved. It's best to think in terms of a unique prospect's unique problem, not in terms of "features" and "benefits" you've memorized before even meeting the person. People do not buy because of a technically-designed feature or a marketing-defined benefit. They buy because of the gap between where they are and where they want to be.

People have lots of problems, but the ones they take action on are the painful ones. Salespeople sometimes think pain is some mystical concept that only a mind reader can identify. Wrong! Whenever you hear comments from prospects like, "I'm embarrassed to X," or "I don't feel safe whenever Y," or "I'm really upset about Z," they're in pain. Your job is to get them to the point that they're comfortable talking about the pain.

> **When they say...**
> ...I don't feel safe...
> ...we keep having problems with...
> ...my neighbors have...
> ...we can't sell our house without...
> ...I'm embarrassed to...
> ...I'm concerned about...
> ...I'm frustrated...
> ...I'm unhappy with...
> ...I'm worried that...
> ...they're in pain!

THE CUSTOMER ISN'T ALWAYS RIGHT

In the world of in-home sales, another factor to consider that is often overlooked in traditional training programs is that prospects may not be experienced at buying the products and services you sell.

It's one thing for people to buy cereal or soap or air freshener at the grocery store. They've purchased these thousands of times before, and they are pretty good at evaluating product labels and claims. They usually know a fair price when they see one, too. Prospects don't need a lot of custom information from a salesperson in that environment because they already know how to buy intelligently.

What's more, those types of purchases are seen as low risk. Consumers think, "I'll try this new sponge," or "The package says it's concentrated, so I can use less. I guess I'll try it." If consumers are unhappy with that decision, they can simply take the product back and request a refund—or forget about a bad investment of a few dollars and try something else the next time.

Homeowners making major improvement/repair decisions face a much more complex situation. For one thing, they likely have social pain that requires spending significant amounts of money but can only be revealed through discussion. You cannot observe a family's home or see their lifestyle to make a judgment about their pain. One homeowner may be disgusted with his two-car garage because he perceives it as small, cramped and overflowing with stored junk. Another person may view a one-car garage as more than adequate and even as the showpiece of the home.

Experience is another issue. Homeowners typically don't know what is important when purchasing an air conditioner, or new windows, or landscape design, or (insert whatever it is you sell here). They may never have purchased your product in their entire life. They may be scared to death of making a mistake, and they may be worried about the "slick salesperson" who is, they are certain, trying to take them to the cleaners.

Remember, a bad purchasing decision in the arenas where you sell may have grave and lasting consequences. Homeowners aren't able to buy a new roof and try it out for a couple of years to decide whether they got a good deal and a quality product. If they make a mistake in their purchasing decision, they may be paying for it for years.

Some of the in-home sales companies that we train prefer to meet with prospects who have made a poor buying choice in the past when working with another vendor. Those prospects are much more knowledgeable about the pitfalls of buying on price alone and are much more aware of the potential implications of sleazy sales tactics. They're more willing to talk about what they've learned, too.

PROSPECTS WANT TO BUY—THEY JUST DON'T WANT TO BE SOLD

Think about your own experience as a customer. You don't want a salesperson to tell you what to do. Odds are that you don't wake up in the morning praying that someone will give you a long lecture about product features either.

The effective salesperson's main objective is not to intimidate, teach or explain. It's to find out whether this prospect is likely to buy. You learn that information through questioning strategies that encourage prospects to talk. They will buy from someone who understands what is important to them and then can explain (in simple terms) how Product X or Service Y will solve their problems.

Liking is not the same as trusting. The fact that prospects like you doesn't hurt the sale, but it also does not mean they will buy from you. They need to trust that you can solve their problems—and make their pain go away.

WHY PEOPLE DON'T BUY

David Sandler figured out that prospects choose not to buy for one, two or all three of the following reasons:

1. The salesperson didn't uncover a problem that the product or service solved.
2. The prospect didn't have enough money to pay for the solution.

3. The prospect wasn't capable of making a decision.

No pain, no money or no decision-making ability means no sale. Everyone hates rejection. It's human nature. What salespeople may fail to recognize is that there is a percentage of prospects who are just not going to buy from them. Rather than invest time estimating, presenting or following up with everyone they meet, they should figure out for themselves whether one or more of the reasons not to buy are present.

If even one of the three issues above linger, you need to accept that having the best product, the greatest sales presentation in history and the best price on earth will not close the sale.

IS THE PROSPECT QUALIFIED?

When prospects are "qualified," it means they have a problem you can fix, they are willing and able to make an investment to solve the problem and they have the power to make the decision to buy. Rather than hope these crucial topics will come up during your discussion, you can and should be proactive in discovering them.

LEAD WHEN YOU DANCE

The Sandler Selling System will help you become more efficient in your selling process and let you lead instead of follow in the Buyer-Seller Dance. Here is an overview of the process:
1. Create rapport.
2. Establish an Up-Front Contract.
3. Let prospects explain their compelling, emotional reason to buy (pain).

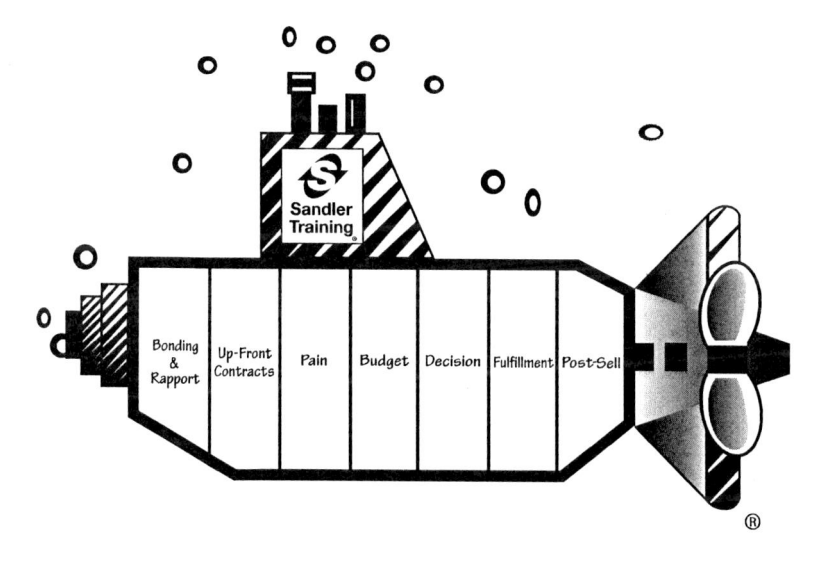

[Diagram: Sandler Submarine with compartments labeled: Bonding & Rapport, Up-Front Contracts, Pain, Budget, Decision, Fulfillment, Post-Sell]

4. Agree to a budget range the prospects are willing to spend.
5. Understand the prospects' decision-making ability and preferences.
6. Provide a presentation tailored to what you learned in the steps above (what is important to the prospects).
7. Re-confirm the sale, manage customer expectations and ask for introductions (referrals).

Why did David Sandler use a submarine to depict the seven parts of the selling system? First, while the Sandler Selling System is a vehicle to get you to your destination, it moves out of sight, below the surface. Please don't tell a prospect, "Mr. Byington, I am going to go through a selling system with you now, so hold on tight. This won't hurt a bit." Remember, unlike a plane or a car, this submarine should not be visible. Second, submarines have compartments. When one compartment fills up with water, you can seal it off and safely move to the next compartment. The compartments are separate parts, each with a different purpose.

Finally, each compartment is in a specific and very important order. Don't use the Pain Step, then the Fulfillment Step and then try the Bonding & Rapport Step. A submarine has a single walkway throughout, so you must travel from one specific section to the next. There are no detours or shortcuts in a submarine, and there shouldn't be any in your selling either.

Consider how differently Mike's visit might have turned out if he had followed this process.

Mike could have started by asking more questions about why the homeowners were replacing the flooring in the first place. (This would likely have uncovered the four-weeks-to-market timeline). He would have had both spouses in attendance because he would have asked up front, on the phone, about the best time to meet with Mrs. Doyle and her husband. He might even have known the real estate agent in question. If he had replaced wood flooring for this agent in the past, he'd have an advantage. One way or another, he could have found out about the budget, the timeline and the relevant pain before presenting a clear option that solved the problems within the budget and on time. At that point, he is no longer selling. He is allowing the prospect to do the buying.

Mike: "Based on what you've seen, what do you see as the next step?"

The Doyles: "Well, can you start installation next week?"

Mike didn't have to be cheaper than the competition, run a special, or have better service and selection than the other guys. He didn't have to attempt a "hard close." He didn't have to get the manager on the phone because there would have been zero price resistance. All he had to do was listen, respond and get out of the way. Icing on the cake? He would now have a much higher closing ratio.

KEY TAKEAWAYS

- If you fail to follow a system, the buyer will control the process.
- Most people buy emotionally, but they justify their decision intellectually.
- People don't buy because of features or benefits; they buy to solve their problems (pain).
- Following a system will allow you to qualify or disqualify a prospect, instead of using "hopium."
- Using the steps of the Sandler Selling System will enable you to allow the prospect to do the buying.

In the next chapter, you will discover how first impressions can make or break your business.

CHAPTER TWO

Voice-to-Voice—
First Impressions Matter

People form a first impression of you and your organization within the first 8–15 seconds of any discussion. That means the person answering the phone has a huge impact on whether or not your salespeople get an appointment.

VOICE-TO-VOICE

Consider this. Your phone is ringing.

That means you and your team have invested significant amounts of time, attention and money in prospecting, getting referrals, securing advertising and using social media effectively. Last but certainly not least, you have vowed to provide excellent service to your clients, so those clients will buy from you repeatedly and refer you to everyone they know.

Congratulations. All your hard work has paid off. The phone is ringing!

Now what?

Well, all too often, this happens:

[Ring, ring.]

"*Perfectly Posh Pools.*"

"Oh, hi, we are looking at getting a pool this summer and I wanted to get a bid."

"OK, can you hold for a moment?"

"Sure."

[Pause for 90 seconds.]

"Can I get your name?"

"Jim Poolbuyer."

"What part of town are you in?"

"Ritzy Falls."

"What's your number?"

"999-555-1212"

"What's your email address?"

"That would be Jim, J-I-M, at moneyisnoobject.com. Need me to spell that again?"

"No, I got it. Now, this is our busy time so it may take a day or two, but someone will call you and set up a time to meet."

"OK, thanks."

Two questions. First, how do you think that went? Second,

how close was that to the first conversation your prospective customers experience when they call your company?

Many new Sandler clients have no major problem with the conversation you just read. They say things like, "The person took the number, and even got an email address (which most people don't do) and set the expectation that it may be a day or two before the prospect gets a call back. It's not great, maybe, but it's acceptable."

Was your reaction anything close to that? If so, it's time for a reality check. If this is the kind of first impression a customer has of your company, you're in trouble. Consider the following points:

1. **That customer may immediately call a few more pool companies.** Jim had the pool on his mind when he dialed your number, but there was no appointment set and certainly nothing that conveyed any good reason for him to wait a couple of days for someone from your company to call. If you were Jim, wouldn't you keep dialing until you had a meaningful discussion with someone and set an appointment that fit your schedule?
2. **That customer is still a complete mystery to you.** You don't know what made Jim call today, and you shouldn't pretend that you do. Jim's motivations might be the same as your marketing methods suggest, or they might be totally different. Imagine all the different possibilities.

    - Maybe Jim decided he is not moving for a while, and he wants a pool installed for his kids by the time summer starts. Maybe he saw a sign in his subdivision with your company's name on it. (Score one for keeping signs up in the consumer's yard as you're working on a project!)

- Maybe Jim's longtime friend Bill gave him your company's name as the best pool builder in town. Maybe Jim invested a couple of hours on the Internet, evaluated all the local companies he could find, and decided his friend was probably right. Then he called you. (A warm referral—even better!)
- Maybe Jim did a "cold" Internet search and liked what he saw about your company.
- Maybe Jim wants to get a quote because he and his wife are hoping to sell their home; the people looking at the property keep asking about how much it might cost to move the trees and install a pool. They want to be able to say a number that sounds realistic. (They may not be the ones buying. You may have to alert your salesperson about the dangers of doing a lot of work up front without a commitment from them or from the potential buyers.)

3. **You just missed an opportunity to engage with Jim, which may have left him with such a bad impression that he won't buy from you.** Face it. There was no engagement that would make Jim want to do business with your company—or even have another discussion. When customers start talking about what made them pick up the phone and dial your number or why they are interested in your product or service, they are more likely to set an appointment. If all they are asked for is contact information, there is no "warm fuzzy" feeling.

4. **Your people weren't trained properly.** When calls like the one you just read happen, it's because there has obviously been no training on a template or script that gets the caller to talk and move to an appointment.

5. **You just made an endless round of phone tag more likely.** Phone tag on calls like this for in-home selling companies is a common outcome. This results in many lost opportunities. Often, companies don't even track these calls well enough to figure out how many are falling through the cracks. Someone in the field gets a message and leaves Jim a voicemail a day or two later, by which time Jim may have already lined up four or five other appointments or gotten frustrated because when he called your team member back, he got voicemail.

The bottom line is this: The best companies learn how to "strike when the iron is hot." They set the appointment on the first call, and then use email to continue the conversation and avoid losing opportunities.

HERE'S WHAT SHOULD MAKE YOU WORRY

What happens when the least trained, least informed person in the entire company picks up the phone and says, "Risky Roofing, can you hold?"

If you're not worrying about that—you should be!

Remember: This is the first real human contact a prospect has with your company. The outcome of this conversation will have a huge impact on your company's probability of winning the caller as a customer. You've invested a lot of time and money to create the circumstance in which this prospect is reaching out to you. Make sure you are doing everything possible to set your company up for success.

Have you heard of the companies that call the employee who answers the phone "Director of First Impressions"? Those companies take the first voice-to-voice contact with a customer seriously—and you should, too. Whether you decide to change people's job titles to reflect their weighty responsibilities (and in our view you should), you must certainly acknowledge that the person who fields these calls is handling all the responsibilities of an inside sales position. At Sandler, we call the first person who speaks to prospects and customers on the phone an "inside salesperson." Feel free to use that term in your organization, too.

Of course, the inside salesperson answering the phone must speak clearly and be a good listener. A friendly, engaging, professional tonality, not phony or condescending, is equally essential. Imagine the voice you would want to hear if you were about to entrust your home to a contractor—perhaps with a large investment. Is that what your prospects are hearing?

A CHECKLIST IS NOT AN EXCUSE FOR AN INTERROGATION

Sometimes business owners hear us make these points and respond by saying, "OK, give me a script—a list of questions my people can use."

While we do recommend a checklist of information to assist the inside salesperson, it always comes with a word of warning. Instead of conducting an inquisition right at the beginning of the relationship, your inside salesperson should let prospects talk about what is on their minds. There is time to get to the questions, but the first few minutes of the call should be considered the prospects' opportunity to talk about what's most important to them. The inside salesperson is there to facilitate that and should show a genuine interest in the prospects' issues.

YOU CAN'T SELL 'EM IF YOU CAN'T TALK TO 'EM

There are no two ways about it. Your best-case scenario on incoming calls from potential customers is to answer the phone.

At the very least, you should make it a priority to return voicemails quickly, but picking up the phone when they call is a much better bet that will give you a significant competitive advantage. People who feel good about their call with your company are more likely to buy from you. Period.

When homeowners get voicemail instead of a real, live human being, there is a much higher likelihood of these unfortunate outcomes:

1. They feel ignored and don't even leave a message. (Ouch.)
2. They feel ignored but do leave a message. (If you think this is happening 100% of the time, you're wrong.)

Even a homeowner who leaves a message has had a negative experience. Why? Because there was no contact with a fellow human being. So, they feel ignored and will call someone else. (This is definitely happening right now if you don't answer your phone lines.)

If you're the homeowner, the inside salesperson's goal is to make you feel like you are the only person calling that day.

Information gathering is the single most important responsibility of the inside salesperson, and prospects don't share information if they feel uncomfortable about the person to whom they're speaking. What the prospect shares in these few minutes is almost always useful later on in the call.

When an opening to ask questions does come along, the inside salesperson should inquire about the homeowner's project or problems before doing anything else. The idea is to get homeowners to explain why they've called.

It's extremely important to resist the temptation to go right into a checklist of standard questions—name, address, how they heard about your company, and so on—right off the bat. A simple example of a better early question might be: "What made you decide to call us today?" This will probably help you uncover how they found you—and the reason they picked up the phone.

HELPING THE CALLER

Your people do need to have a list of multiple-choice responses in case the homeowner struggles to explain why he or she is calling. If all your inside salesperson hears is what the homeowner wants to have done, it's time to pose one of those well-designed multiple-choice questions. Here's an example of what such a question would sound like: "Normally when people call us, it's because a room is too hot or too cold, a unit isn't working that affects the entire house or there is a loud or unusual noise. Is any of that happening?"

Once your inside salesperson has obtained information about

what made the homeowner call that day, it is appropriate to ask the homeowner for a name. This request could sound like this: "By the way, my name is Chris. I don't believe I wrote down your name." Prospects will most likely then give theirs. From this point forward, questions about where the prospects live, whether or not prospects own their homes, when prospects would like to see someone and so on will all come quite naturally. The important thing is to open the call by showing some interest in the caller's concerns.

You want to make sure that if there are two decision makers, they both are present at the meeting if possible. Always ask in a way that implies other customers have both people at the meeting and includes a WIIFT (what's in it for them). Here is an example:

"Bob, typically when I work with other couples, both of them want to be at our initial appointment. That way, I can answer all of their questions at the same time. Many times each person has a different perspective and wants different information before deciding whether or not to move forward with this type of project. And, it is OK if we are not the right solution for you. Either way, we can decide then if there is any reason to get more information or move to the next step in the process. How does next Wednesday look?"

We used "typically" to imply that most people agree to this on our initial appointment, and we gave a couple of reasons it is to their benefit to be there. Finally, we used the tools in our up-front contract to reinforce that they can say "no," which adds credibility and makes them more likely to agree.

UQ VS. OQ

Companies that do in-home selling generally fall into two camps when it comes to interacting with prospects.

- Camp One: Any time a homeowner contacts the company, the company sends someone out. This is called under-qualifying, or UQ.
- Camp Two: When the homeowner calls, the inside salesperson asks lots of probing questions, including how much the prospect can spend, and may even try to figure out if the homeowner will buy from the company before agreeing to send someone out. This is called over-qualifying, or OQ.

The UQers usually swear they "just want the appointment" and that nothing of consequence can possibly be accomplished on the phone. The OQers say the cost of sending someone out on such visits is prohibitively high, and they fear spending too much time creating estimates that don't win the business.

Our message for the UQers is that there is much, much more that can be done to improve closing and conversion rates by taking an extra few minutes on the phone and coordinating strategies with the salesperson.

What about the OQers? In our experience, the only way to convince these folks to change is for them to measure the increased revenue that occurs as a result of following this book's advice and compare those figures to the slightly increased cost of sales that accompanies a decision to go out on a sales call. As you'll see in later pages of this book, the fact that you visit a homeowner doesn't mean you have to give a bid. That realization alone will help reduce your cost of sales.

We have seen OQ home improvement companies increase their annual revenues by 35 to 40% just by doing less stringent qualifying on the phone and a handful of additional techniques in person. What the OQers typically don't understand is that large-ticket sales require face-to-face interactions, not voice-to-voice, to close.

Consider this: Big online retailers know the difference between online shopping carts, voice-to-voice and face-to-face. That's why they haven't tried to take over the in-home sales market. Most homeowners won't be buying a new solar-panel system, adding an outdoor kitchen or landscaping their backyard via online giants anytime soon. Don't give your voice-to-voice and face-to-face advantage away by poorly qualifying on the phone.

TO BUDGET OR NOT TO BUDGET?

One particularly controversial topic is discussing cost or cost brackets with a prospect on the phone before any salesperson arrives. Sandler is clear on this point: Get an ounce of pain and then go for the appointment!

The inside salesperson must understand that each homeowner has certain problems that need attention. You don't have to find out everything about your prospect from a single phone call—just enough to know the particular pain. Once it is evident that a problem you can solve is present, the inside salesperson should book the appointment.

The inside salesperson who is properly trained may choose to ask homeowners whether they have a budget, but that should be the extent of a discussion about budget or money on the phone. There is no need to inquire about actual dollar amounts.

For the OQers out there, this may be a leap of faith. No, you don't want to appear too eager to meet with prospects. Yet the reality is that over-qualifying doesn't pay in the long run. Even if you have a waiting list of clients after employing the concepts in this book, do not over-qualify on the phone. You'll have a much better chance of convincing someone to wait to work with your company if you build up face-to-face trust. Don't forget the importance of face-to-face selling utilizing all the techniques described throughout this book.

IT'S NOT A DEMOCRACY—IT'S BUSINESS

The information the inside salesperson gathers is important. Not only will this information be useful to the salesperson during face-to-face discussions, it should also be used to prioritize appointments. One in-home sales team determined they had a higher closing ratio in a particular subdivision with rules that favored their product specifications. Another learned through tracking that they had a better close ratio with homeowners who drove BMWs. One window company found it had a higher close ratio with homes that were over 60 years old in specific neighborhoods.

Some pieces of customer data matter more to your business than others. Teach your inside salesperson to uncover these nuggets of information. Your salespeople will appreciate it. You may choose to give high-value homeowners higher priority in your appointment scheduling. By the same token, the data will also tell you that some prospects are likelier to be tougher to close. Identify who those are and prioritize them accordingly. If you can systematically identify the tough price shoppers, maybe those are the folks to refer to your competition.

> **Not all prospects are meant to be customers!**

When you find that a prospect does not qualify to become a customer, close the file and move on. Train your inside salesperson with the principle that just because a homeowner asks for an appointment, that doesn't mean it is required to book one. When a homeowner doesn't have a problem that your company fixes, you could also refer them to a strategic partner who may be able to help.

KNOW WHAT TO ASK THE PROSPECT TO DO

Yes, there are many prospects who are hard to close. These prospects require care and careful application of specific techniques to manage them through the buying cycle. But have you ever calculated how many salespeople unintentionally prevent the customer from buying even when they are ready? It's a substantial number.

Consider the case of the prospect who has already told the inside person that he is ready to make a decision. In this case, your outside salesperson must bring a contract to the meeting. If he doesn't, he will prolong the sale and may even frustrate the ready-to-buy prospect for making the process take more time than planned. The homeowner was ready to buy, and the salesperson wouldn't let him!

A client of ours once observed, "Time kills deals." Truer words were never spoken. An extended sales cycle is sure to add time and reduce the likelihood of a successful close. Make sure your inside salespeople share all the relevant information with the salesperson.

Before we move on, here is a different way to handle that call from Jim, the prospect who was interested in a new pool.

Kathy: "Perfectly Posh Pools, this is Kathy. May I help you?"

Jim: "Yes, I was calling to get a bid on a new pool."

Kathy: "Great. What made you decide to call us today?"

Jim "I saw your sign in a neighbor's yard, and we want to get one installed before summer. The kids have been begging for a pool."

Kathy: "Oh? How old are your kids?"

Jim: "Ten and twelve. They think their friends will be over all the time if we have a pool."

Kathy: "It sounds like they are on a mission! What is your name?"

Jim: "Jim Poolbuyer."

Kathy: "Jim, have you decided that this will be the summer to get them a pool?"

Jim: "Well, we think we have budgeted it to get a decent-sized pool installed. I have asked some neighbors and know about what it might cost."

Kathy: "Have you been looking into a certain kind of pool?"

Jim: "I know we want to have a hot tub on the end and for it to be deep enough for a diving board. I haven't met with any other pool companies yet, but when I saw your sign, it made me think it's time to take a serious look at what we might want."

Kathy: "Most of our customers don't know exactly what they want when they first call, and they are looking for someone to help them understand the different options that meet their family's needs and are within their budget. Can I make a suggestion?"

Jim: "Sure."

Kathy: "Typically, we set up an initial meeting at your home that takes about an hour. Our consultant will meet with you and get a general idea of what you may be looking for; they can also share how we have worked with other homeowners in the area. There is no obligation. Then, if you both decide to move forward, you would pay a nominal deposit to begin preliminary design of the pool. How does that sound?"

Jim: "Sounds good. Saturday morning would be best."

Kathy: "I'm guessing your wife will want to be in on that meeting?"

Jim: "Yes, I suppose she would."

Kathy: "Is that a good time for her?"

Jim: "You know what? You better make it Saturday afternoon. She's usually taking the kids to soccer practice on Saturday morning."

Kathy: "Great. Let me get some information from you while I pull up our schedule."

This initial engagement was personalized, professional and respectful of the busy homeowner's time. It resulted in a clear next step. The minimal time invested probably prevented the homeowner from making further calls.

When prospects coordinate schedules to invite you into their home, that's a clear sign that they believe you can help solve their problem. If you consistently make it easy for them to set up that kind of an appointment, your sales will increase.

By the way, here is an email template that you might want to use to send as a follow up after an appointment is set.

> Jim,
>
> Great talking with you today. I'm glad to confirm that you and your wife Velma have an appointment with Laura Extraordinaire from Perfectly Posh Pools on Saturday at 3:00 p.m.
>
> Other customers have selected Perfectly Posh Pools because:
>
> - They wanted a local company that could alleviate their concern about selecting the right pool within their budget.
> - They have busy schedules and want a professional company to eliminate any frustration involved in selecting and installing their new pool.
>
> Please call us with any questions. Laura has scheduled approximately one hour to meet with you both and is looking forward to Saturday. By the end of the meeting, you can decide if you'd like to move to the design phase.
>
> I hope Perfectly Posh Pools is part of making your summer a success!
>
> Warmly,
>
> Kathy
>
> Amazing Inside Salesperson

KEY TAKEAWAYS:

- The first few minutes on the phone can be critical to your sales results.
- Ask the right questions that engage the prospects in talking about what is important to them.
- Follow a process to transition to a clear next step (preferably an appointment).
- Invest in the time to train and practice with your inside sales professionals.

In the next chapter, you will learn how to start each appointment with the right approach and set the stage for a successful outcome each time.

CHAPTER THREE

Set the Stage for Success

Most sales are won or lost within the first few minutes in the home.

Perhaps you're nodding your head right now, thinking we're going to say that this is because prospects make quick judgments about salespeople. Or bad first impressions can't be undone. Or buyers who let you into their home do not usually trust salespeople, based on past bad experiences.

All of that is correct. But none of it is the real reason the sale so often self-destructs within a few minutes of the time you walk in the door. The real reason salespeople fail so quickly is that they follow the lead of the prospect, instead of leading the dance themselves.

Let's face it—customers like to control the sales process. They get their pricing emailed to them; they take as much time as they need to "think things over"; they demand a boatload of expertise. Some of them expect salespeople to take the lead in solving the problem, of course, but even so, customers want to control the process on their own terms, and most salespeople give them that control.

Here is a typical example of what we mean.

Chip, an HVAC service technician, knocks on the door of his next appointment. The homeowner, Judy, welcomes him in. Over the course of the (critical) first few minutes, Judy does almost all the talking. But instead of sharing any of her personal concerns, she starts talking about the funny noises her A/C unit has been making.

For his part, Chip nods a lot.

Judy offers to show Chip where the unit is located. She leads him outside.

While they're walking, he asks a few questions about those funny noises. He tells Judy he will take a look, and then track her down.

Judy says she'll be in the kitchen. She goes about her business.

Fifteen minutes later, Chip knocks on the door again and Judy answers. He diagnoses the problem. (Note: Both of them are still standing at the door!)

"Judy," Chip says, "it looks like you may actually need a whole new unit. We can quote that for you. We can also offer a maintenance program to prevent this problem in the future. I can put some pricing together for you that will take only a few minutes."

"Oh," says Judy. "That's nice. Hey, why don't you set up some options, pricing, and all the information, and then send me an email so my husband and I can review it together?"

"Sure," Chip says. He jots down her email address. "I'll get that out to you tonight." He hands Judy a brochure. He remembers the product training he received and manages to get in a few words about his company's great A/C units and how long they have been in business.

Judy says, "You've been very helpful." She thanks him again. She closes the door.

TIME OUT

Would you describe Chip's call as "good" or even "sold"?

How about these questions:

- Are you busy rushing through initial calls to get back to a computer to email quotes?
- Do you have a low closing ratio, no matter how many quotes you send or how much you rush?
- Do you have little time to follow up?
- Is every call you go out on a "good call"?
- Do you have trouble identifying a discussion that has little chance of closing?

Make no mistake. The discussion above is not "good." It's not "promising." It's not "about to close." No matter how many such exchanges he has, no matter how many quotes he emails after initiating this kind of "relationship," Chip has nothing. The customer controlled the entire call. Chip lost the opportunity to have a better outcome within the first few minutes in her home.

At Sandler, we believe the purpose of any initial discussion with a prospect is to identify common barriers to a sale and then to either let the prospect handle those barriers or end the appointment. This is true of any sale in any environment and certainly of in-home selling, where prospects are allowing you into their living space.

What are some of those obstacles?

Probably the biggest potential obstacle in in-home selling is a **lack of trust**. When you enter a home, it is critical that you be seen as a professional and that you gain credibility as quickly as possible.

Having sufficient time for an appointment is certainly a potential issue. If the prospect is feeling rushed and is more focused on some other commitment (such as a football game about to start or friends and family arriving any moment), there is no way to have a constructive discussion about any pain that you might be able to alleviate. Set up another time to talk, or adjust to the time allocated. Understand your options in the first few minutes. Don't get cut short on time.

Another barrier is not **setting a clear purpose and agenda** for the meeting. For example, Chip is coming in to assess a potentially bad A/C unit and possibly a replacement and a maintenance agreement. In order to do that, he will need to sit down with the homeowner; discuss the problems she is having; talk about what access to the unit he will need; gather whatever other information he may need in order to evaluate the possible solutions; and share information that might be important to the homeowner—all before Chip looks at the unit.

A good sales professional will discuss, up front, the **options for the end of the appointment**. This is the best way to find out, early on, whether you are looking at otherwise hidden obstacles. Some examples might be:

- Spouse or other decision maker is not available.
- Competitor is coming in right before or right after you.
- Brother-in-law or other relative who is a novice handyman is coming by later to see if he can install it himself.
- And, the ever-popular, "We are waiting until summer when it really gets hot to make a decision."

These and other potential obstacles are best dealt with proactively. An effective salesperson will bring them up first and address them directly.

In the pages that follow, we will look at many of these in-home selling barriers and show you effective techniques for addressing them and even improving the likelihood of a successful close.

"WHAT KIND OF CONTRACT?"

The first critical technique for uncovering these barriers and increasing the salesperson's closing percentage is called an ***up-front contract***. Even talking about establishing a "contract" at the beginning of a discussion with prospects is often intimidating to salespeople. You might think, *If I haven't even told my prospects why they should buy from me, how am I supposed to get them to agree to a contract?*

Relax. There's nothing for prospects to sign in an up-front contract, and money is not exchanged. In the purest sense of the word, a contract is merely an agreement between two or more people about something that will take place in the future. Confirming whether there will be sufficient time, whether both spouses will attend a meeting, or whether you will have easy access to the relevant areas of the house could be important elements of your up-front contract.

If you look at what best practices are already delivering results for successful in-home salespeople, in or out of your industry, you will usually find that some kind of habitual up-front contract is part of that success.

Many plumbers understand up-front agreements intuitively. When making an appointment with homeowners, they explain that they charge for a service call, that they will estimate additional labor and material costs, and that if the homeowner decides to have the work done by the plumber, they will credit the cost of the service call to the final repair price. All of this usually happens before the plumber steps in the door. Notice that most plumbers are OK with you saying "no" to all of that. That's the sign of a good up-front contract, no matter what you call it.

MAKE IT OK TO SAY "NO"

In his own selling career, much of which involved door-to-door selling, David Sandler learned quickly that one of the major barriers to success was the TIO or "think it over" response. Even if the prospect had an urgent problem, money to spend and the authority to make a decision, he still might say something like, "You are the first person I've spoken to," or "I just want to digest this and give it some thought before making a decision."

Sandler discovered that getting a *no* was OK, getting a *yes* was better, but getting a TIO was deadly. An up-front contract, properly executed, gives the prospect the option to say "no"—and reduces the number of TIOs from your world.

But it's likely that you're wondering: Why would any good salesperson ever bring up the idea that the customer might say "no" to their product or service? There are two reasons.

- First, customers say "no" all the time without permission. They do that in any number of ways. They don't call back; they email that they went with another company; they say they need to "think it over" when they have actually decided they are not going to buy.
- Second, telling them that a *no* is OK builds credibility. Giving them the option to say "no" right out loud makes it much more likely that you'll know what's actually going on in the relationship. It lowers barriers and makes you look like a consultant and not someone desperate to get a sale. Also, a clear *no* from the prospect is actually a very good outcome. The known is better than the unknown.

Successful salespeople know that if they get a decision quickly, they can move on to the next sales call or spend more time prospecting. The salespeople who fail are the ones who follow up and spend too much "checking in" with prospects who didn't make a decision the first time around, and subsequently delay even more. Does that sound even a little familiar? If it does, can you imagine a world where you had much better information about the prospects with whom you chose to invest your precious time?

SANDLER RULE

You can't lose what you don't have!

If a customer does not buy from you, it will never be because you gave him permission to say "no." You never had the sale in the first place. By making it OK to say "no," you might find out the real reason sooner rather than later.

The second reason to offer the *no* option, which is even more important, is that you need to lower barriers between yourself and the prospect. Putting the option to say "no" right out there on the table does that. It makes people feel like they are in control of the process. Salespeople who give the prospect the option to say "no" instantly set themselves apart from the competition. They come across as more credible and they are better at building up trust because they don't seem desperate.

Look again at what Chip did in the previous interaction.

- He didn't confirm how much time was needed for the call. (As a result, he got shortchanged.)
- He allowed the customer to control the entire meeting.
- He missed the chance to sit down with the homeowner, understand her concerns and get other valuable information critical to the sales process.
- He opted instead to focus on technical issues and analyze the mechanical state of the A/C unit. (Another way of saying all this is that he skipped the Pain, Budget, and Decision Steps of the Sandler Selling System.)
- By not sitting down with the customer in the beginning and discussing the homeowner's issues as they appeared to her, he put all the pressure on the later "closing" discussion. Customers have learned how to avoid those.
- He agreed to send an email quote that would easily allow the customer to compare his price against that of the

competition. That puts too much focus on price and leaves him committed to invest even more time trying to close a prospect who has not agreed to any clear next step.
- He accepted the deadly "think it over."

The main reason Chip made all of those mistakes was he was used to making them, over and over again. He thought that was the best way to open the relationship. It isn't. The only question now is: Can Chip learn to adapt to a new way of conducting discussions with prospects?

If you can adapt, lots of new possibilities open up!

A NEW WAY TO OPEN THE DISCUSSION

Suppose Chip had said this instead at the outset of his meeting with Judy:

> "Judy, thank you for inviting me into your home. Do you have about an hour today? That's about how long this typically takes. Great. Now, what usually makes sense is for us to sit down for a few minutes. I'll ask you some questions about the problems you have been having and answer any questions you may have about why other homeowners have chosen our company. Then I'll look at your system and prepare some options that we can sit down and review. By the way, if for some reason we are not the right company for you, it's completely OK to say 'no.' On the other hand, if I find the repair is something I can do while I'm here, you can decide to have me fix it today. If the repair is substantial or you decide to order new equipment, you could choose to make a deposit so we could order it for you. Does that sound OK?"

If Chip had done something like that, he would have avoided every single one of his mistakes. In the second version of this meeting, Chip included all elements of the up-front contract:

- Time
- Purpose
- His agenda/customer's agenda
- Possible outcomes (allowing *no* as a critical component)

Because of this approach, he gained immediate credibility and set the stage for success in this call. As discussed earlier, success can also be finding out someone is not willing and able to buy your product or service. Guess what? Homeowners with a genuine intent to buy appreciate up-front contracts, too.

LOWER THE ANXIETY AND RESPECT THEIR TIME

Homeowners can be expected to have anxiety about the sales process, how they will be treated, whether they will be embarrassed due to their lack of experience and what will happen during and after the appointment. The up-front contract helps to alleviate that anxiety.

Customers who have set an appointment and have a clear and present need for your product or service are unlikely to be "tire kickers." These people are busy. They have made time for you to come into their personal environment and discuss a problem. You should expect that you will have every opportunity to get a sale—if you set the agenda properly.

While you should never use the phrase "up-front contract" with prospects, you should understand that you have a responsibility to set and manage mutual expectations with them prior to the appointment. Most of the time, prospects will welcome this. Good prospects want to buy. They welcome the opportunity to learn about next steps, remove uncertainty and understand how your company's process works. As a rule, Sandler always recommends covering the key elements of the up-front contract before the salesperson arrives at the appointment. This satisfies ready-to-buy prospects so they know what is necessary. It will also clarify next steps with a confused homeowner who may have other expectations. Of course, if a homeowner does not want to make even the smallest decision, it's best for the salesperson to know before going to the appointment. A salesperson might then choose to give other prospects and appointments higher priority.

The phone receptionist or inside salesperson can usually complete an up-front contract without much difficulty. Referring back to the example of Perfectly Posh Pools back on page 36, Kathy was effective in discussing the decision that Jim would need to make at the end of his meeting with the pool salesperson, Laura. Kathy covered all the elements of the up-front contract in her phone conversation with Jim as well as in the follow-up email confirming his appointment with Laura.

MIRRORING AND MATCHING

Another important way to set the stage for success is to make your prospects comfortable the moment you enter their home. This is bonding and rapport—but it is different from establishing bonding and rapport in the way you might have been taught.

Often salespeople will immediately offer a compliment or try to find a common interest when they go into a sales call. The problem is that sometimes prospects don't know why you are talking about the weather, their kids' pictures or that recent sporting event. This "small talk" often backfires, leaving you further away from that feeling of mutual trust you want to instill.

Some people will want to get right to the point about why you were contacted, and others may want to spend some time talking about other things. Some people will immediately withdraw if they feel they have encountered a "fast talking" sales professional or someone they believe gives them a disingenuous compliment as a way to get to a sale. In reality, there is more to bonding and rapport than making small talk about how nice the surroundings are. Learning how to adapt to your prospect is much more important.

OBSERVE YOUR PROSPECT

In actual practice, salespeople must find ways to build rapport and trust quickly with each and every prospect they meet. This means taking a customized approach. Personality and communication styles are very important clues on how to best build rapport and put prospects at ease. There is no "one best way" to communicate with a prospect.

Numerous studies have shown that people tend to prefer communication styles that closely match their own. For example, if prospects talk slowly, they will feel more comfortable with a salesperson who speaks slowly. If prospects speak with detailed and descriptive language, they will be more comfortable with a salesperson who uses detailed and descriptive language.

People buy from people with whom they feel comfortable. Unfortunately, all prospects are not like you. Yes, there are certain types of people and personal styles that you probably connect with immediately. You can tell that these prospects get along with people like you. You know that this connection will increase your chances of closing a sale if they have the problems that your company is good at fixing.

On the other hand, there are certain prospects who have the problems you are great at fixing but their communication style is very different than your own. You know they should probably buy from your company after some detailed questioning, but the connection isn't there. They may purchase from a competitor simply because they feel more comfortable with the other company.

Here are some common examples of when salespeople fail to adapt:

- Salespeople start every call with the same approach: they look around the home and talk about something ("How old are your children?") or they talk about themselves. The prospect wants to get to the point of the meeting.
- The prospect is detail-oriented but the salesperson is not. The prospect asks a specific question, but the salesperson glosses over it and moves on.
- Married prospects want to talk about how the carpet stains are from when their son was a baby, but now he is about to start kindergarten. The salesperson acts disinterested and quickly moves to selecting a color.
- The salesperson talks very fast and jumps in anytime there is brief silence. The prospects are more reserved and are suspicious about being "sold."

You may not be connecting with everyone as you should. This chapter offers some strategies that will help you improve your connection skills—and make it easier for you to set up-front contracts and sustain bonding and rapport throughout the sales process.

VISUAL MATCHING

Your body posture gives subtle messages to your prospects, as does theirs to you. For example, if a prospect is standing, you know it would seem awkward for you to sit.

You can match your prospects with many aspects of body posture. If they are leaning forward at a table, you can lean forward. If they have their arms crossed, it is best to cross your arms, too. If they are smiling, you should smile. If they are leaning back in a relaxed pose, you should, too. Simply becoming aware of your own body posture is useful as it's not unusual to get nervous or overly excited on a sales call. Matching your prospects' body posture has been shown to be an effective way of putting people at ease.

VERBAL MATCHING

If your prospects speak quickly, you should, too. If they speak slowly, it would be best to slow down. If they speak loudly, they may perceive you are unsure if you speak softly. If they speak softly, they may feel you are imposing and intimidating if you speak loudly.

The majority of your communication is linked to your body posture and tonality. For instance, you could say, "You have a lovely home," but if your body language, facial expression and tonality indicate you really think otherwise, you could get off to a bad start on a sales call. Salespeople often don't appreciate how every facial expression and tone they use is sending strong and sometimes unintended messages to their prospects.

Using the words prospects use and keeping explanations and terms simple can help prospects feel more at ease. Sales professionals tend to use buzzwords that may make prospects uncomfortable. Industry terms, abbreviations and complex names may come across as talking over people's heads and thus jeopardize the sale.

For example, if you sell windows and your prospect calls the grilles across the windows "cross bars," then you will put him at ease if you use the term "cross bar." While you may normally say "divided light" or "grilles," prospects may be confused or feel you are not listening to them if you use different phrases.

If prospects use the term "stovetop," refrain from calling it a "cooktop." If they call it "carpet," avoid the term "floor covering." If they tell you they have dry rot in the "overhang," this is not the time to correct them and explain it is actually a "soffit." Simply say, "Could we look at the overhang together?" or any appropriate response, making sure to incorporate their phrases.

COMMUNICATION STYLES

One of the important areas of training we conduct at Sandler is in the area of communication styles. People are more likely to buy from you when you mirror their communication style. However, with in-home selling, often you are dealing with two different customers and therefore two different communication styles. You need to be able to adapt to both.

You may wonder how you can identify each person's communication style quickly in order to match and mirror effectively. There are four basic communication styles, which are combinations of the following two categories. With a little practice, you can decipher someone's style within a couple of minutes.

People tend to be either more reserved or more active communicators.

Active communicators may also be seen as extroverted. Their thoughts are not necessarily "screened" and are easily shared. If you are naturally more reserved, you typically speak more slowly and, to you, pauses or silence between words are natural. You may think through ideas before sharing, especially with someone you have recently met.

If you are naturally more reserved and your customers are more active, you may need to adapt your rate of speech and level of interaction to mirror their style. You may also need to allow more time for their thoughts and opinions to be expressed. Decisions are typically made more quickly with active communicators, so be careful not to draw out a presentation or sales process when your customer may be ready to make a decision much earlier in the sales call.

If you are a more active communicator and your customers are more reserved, you may need to slow down your rate of speech and ask more questions to draw out their opinions. Allow time to answer questions thoroughly and be comfortable with some silence during the sales call.

People tend to be more facts/task-oriented or more people/emotions-oriented.

If you are more facts/task-oriented, you may focus on achieving the goal of the meeting objective. You may want to get down to business quickly. If you are facts-oriented and reserved, you may like details and be inclined to share a large amount of product information. If your customers, however, are more people/emotions-oriented communicators, they may want to have time for light conversation and need you to listen to stories about people they know or personal experiences. Overwhelming them with details may cause you to lose the sale.

By contrast, if you are more people/emotions-oriented, you may want to reference stories or examples that involve people or give more information about feelings. If your customers are more facts-oriented, you may need to limit personal stories and conversation in order for them to be comfortable with you.

Here is a basic grid with the four primary communication styles in combination.

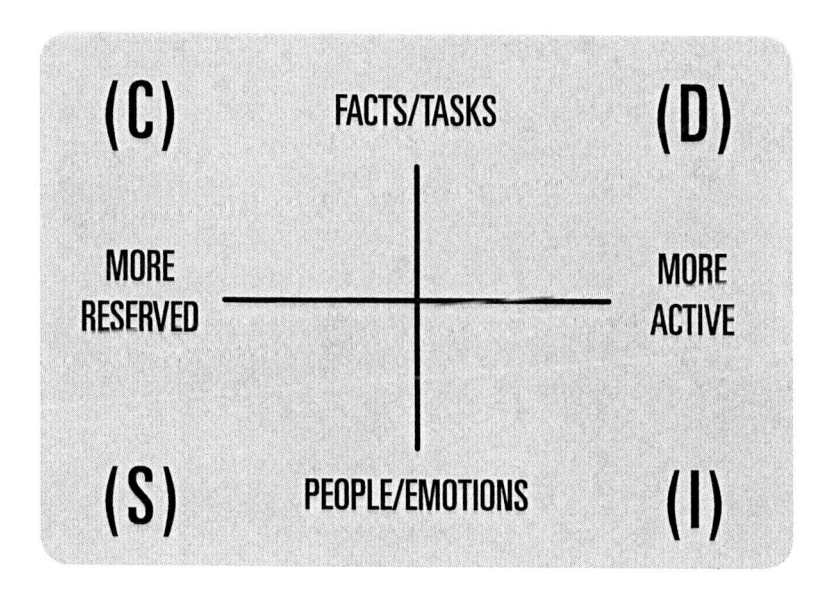

```
(C)         FACTS/TASKS          (D)
                 |
                 |
   MORE          |              MORE
 RESERVED  ——————+——————       ACTIVE
                 |
                 |
(S)        PEOPLE/EMOTIONS       (I)
```

Sandler emphasizes a system of evaluating communication styles called DISC. DISC assessments and training help salespeople to first understand their own primary communication style and then learn how to quickly adapt to their prospects' styles in order to make them more comfortable. You can receive your own customized report that can help you practice adapting quickly as you interact with prospects. Contact your local Sandler trainer or go to www.Sandler.com for more details.

Now that you see a general overview of each style, here are ways you can learn to identify and adapt in order to make your prospects more comfortable.

How to Identify C-Style
- Precise, exact, analytical
- Logical, systematic
- Quiet, does not express emotions
- Careful, formal, disciplined
- Focuses on details; asks many questions
- Deliberate and controlled
- Well prepared; may have done homework
- Not comfortable with physical contact
- Studies specifications/info carefully
- May be very critical; criticism based on facts, not opinions
- Makes decisions only after studying pertinent facts/issues

How to Identify D-Style
- Decisive, tough, impatient
- Strong-willed, competitive
- Demanding, independent
- Direct, does not listen
- Appears to be in a hurry
- Says what he/she thinks; may be blunt
- States own opinions as facts
- Interrupts others
- "What's the bottom line?"
- "How does this benefit ME?"
- Becomes irritated easily

How to Identify S-Style
- Calm, steady, laid-back
- Caring, patient, amiable
- Listens carefully, sincere
- Modest, indecisive, trustworthy
- Listens carefully, nods and goes along
- Appears thoughtful
- "Let me think about it."
- Likes own physical space
- Ponders options, slow making decisions
- Seems to have strong opinions but does not express them vocally
- Completely new ideas/things seem to make him/her uncomfortable

How to Identify I-Style
- Sociable, talkative, open
- Enthusiastic, energetic
- Persuasive, spontaneous, impulsive
- Emotional, talks more than listens
- Is animated
- Talks about people he/she knows
- Does not focus much on details
- Does not listen for long
- May ask same questions several times
- Jumps from subject to subject
- Stays away from hard facts

© 1997-2015 Extended DISC N.A., Inc.   All Rights reserved. "Extended DISC" is a registered trademark of Extended DISC N.A., Inc.

How to Communicate with C-style

- Use data and facts
- Examine an argument from all sides
- Keep on task; proceed logically
- Disagree with the facts, not the person
- Focus on quality
- Avoid untested solutions; use proven ideas
- Respect personal space
- Be patient, slow down
- Do not talk about personal issues
- Explain carefully

How to Communicate with D-style

- Be direct, brief, and to the point
- Focus on the task; stick to business
- Use a results-oriented approach
- Identify opportunities/challenges
- Ensure he/she wins
- Offer solutions and alternatives
- Touch on high points; don't overuse data
- Be aware of personal space
- Do not be emotional, do not dominate
- Act quickly, he/she decides fast

How to Communicate with S-style

- Be patient, build trust
- Draw out his/her opinions
- Present issues logically
- Relax; allow time for discussions
- Show how solutions will benefit him/her
- Clearly define responsibilities
- Involve him/her in planning
- Slow down your approach
- Provide the information he/she needs
- Secure commitment step by step

How to Communicate with I-style

- Allow time for socializing
- Lighten up; have fun
- Ask for feelings and opinions
- Smile and be animated
- Create a fun environment
- Be friendly and warm, do not ignore
- Express enthusiasm
- Let him/her speak
- Give recognition
- Speak about people and feelings

SPOT THE SIGNALS EARLY

The communication preference evaluation process can start with the first phone call to your office, but all too often, it doesn't. Here is an example of mismatched communication styles in an initial conversation.

Customer: "Hi there. I got your name from my neighbor Wanda Bye here in the Greenback subdivision. I'd like to get a quote on your alarms."

Inside Salesperson: "OK."

Customer: "So how does it work exactly? Do I need to describe my home and how many sensors I want for my alarm?"

Inside Salesperson: "I just need your address and your name."

Customer: "My name is Jillian Maxwell De La Hoya and we live on 25 Sunny Brook Lane, which is about one block from the Big Bell Breakfast restaurant, which we own."

Inside Salesperson: "Got it. And when would you like to see someone about a security system?"

Customer: "What's a security system?"

Inside Salesperson: "It's an alarm."

Customer: "Oh I see. Well, I've been thinking about that. I guess it really depends on how long it takes to order and install one. Obviously sooner is better than later. We have been having break-ins in the area and..."

Inside Salesperson: [interrupting] "How about Wednesday at 1:00 P.M.?"

What's going wrong? The inbound salesperson is not matching communication styles with the homeowner, who is obviously a more active communicator for whom social connection is important. Also, using words like "security system" instead of "alarm" doesn't help. This homeowner wants to share information, but the salesperson is not engaged—or interested.

This happens too often with in-home selling. It happens on the phone, and it also happens when the salespeople go into the home. They are often dealing with two different people, each with a different communication style. Why does this matter? Because when you fail to adapt to the prospect, you may lose a sale before you even start the process.

If you detect that you are dealing with someone more direct, then get to the point. Match this style and keep the discussion around results. If your prospect is more reserved and detail-oriented and is criticizing an aspect of the home and doing calculations on a calculator, don't distract him or interrupt his thoughts. First recognize your own tendencies, and then become aware of how you can adapt to the prospect's tendencies.

Alter your words, tone, body posture and external behaviors to each person as you communicate with each one. If you begin conversing with another person, even in the same room, alter your communication accordingly. With a little time and practice, you will be able to have comfortable rapport-building conversations with almost anyone.

KEY TAKEAWAYS:

- Set the purpose/agenda.
- Don't get cut short on time.
- Find out barriers up front within the first few minutes.
- Allowing *no* as an option will build trust and reduce "think it overs."
- Know how to adapt your communication style to make your prospect comfortable.

Now picture this: You are sitting down with the customer. You are up to bat. In the next chapter, you will learn how to ask the right questions to discover what is important to him. That's when the real magic begins!

CHAPTER FOUR

Could Asking Questions Be the Answer?

True or false: Selling only happens when the prospect is talking. We hope you said, "True!"

But have you ever heard anyone say anything like the following?

"He can talk to anybody. He should be in sales."

"In sales, a *no* doesn't mean 'no'; it just means the prospect needs more information."

"She is so outgoing; she talks a mile a minute. She would be great selling our product."

These are some of the common misconceptions people have about what makes someone a so-called "born salesperson." All of them are rooted in the fallacy that talking is the same thing as moving a sale forward. It's not. Great salespeople know how to ask good questions, and they know how to make sure the prospect does most of the talking.

But that's generally not what happens. Here is a typical in-home sales example.

The salesperson, who didn't read the previous chapter, compliments the prospect's nice house and spends a few minutes chatting about the beautiful weather. Then he gets down to business.

"Let me tell you a little about Super Security Systems. We have the very best alarm system in the industry. We have been in the business for over 20 years, and we are a leader in the market. We have the most up-to-date technology, and our support center is state of the art. We are always responsive; we make sure that you have peace of mind when you are away."

The salesperson takes a breath, finally, and pulls out a sample keypad and brochure.

"Here is one of our newest, super-duper keypads. You gotta love those color-coded buttons, right? Think how great it will look as a wall accessory. We have a great special going on today. If you sign up, we will include motion sensors, lasers and a cool, disco strobe light. I can go ahead and write everything up for you and include the promotion and extra keypad. I will also be happy to leave one of our brochures, which explains how the buttons/system work. I also take pride in making sure I provide excellent customer service, and I will make sure everything goes smoothly. If you sign today, we can install on either Tuesday or Thursday. Which of those is best for you?"

You may be thinking that sounds pretty good. He covered how long the company had been in the business, and he walked the prospect through all the great technology. He pulled out a sample and showed the customer exactly how it would look. He gave a closing incentive—and added some excitement with that cool disco light! He even offered a choice of dates to install the system.

Here's the problem: Remember that the customer hears the same "spiel" from other vendors so it all sounds the same. Standardized pitches mean that your customers hear the same things from your competitors when they are considering the purchase of a product or service like yours. They hear: "We have great products; great service; and oh, by the way, I am pretty great and will take care of you." They hear that on almost any sales presentation about anything. So, if you sound the same, they may put you in the same category.

There's also another problem. The salesperson has no idea if any of the supposed benefits he mentioned are perceived to be of value by the prospect. Perhaps a few of those pearls are of interest, but just because you categorize them as benefits does not mean they are benefits in the prospect's opinion. He might think, *All those buttons look complicated, don't they? And security when I'm away? No, no, I want to be secure when I am home! This product doesn't apply to me.* "Mr. Salesperson, thank you for your time. I am just looking..."

Uh oh.

DIFFERENTIATING YOURSELF

The question is, how can you differentiate yourself when your competitors are likely to present themselves with the same or a similar product as yours, equally great service and pricing that may even be lower than yours?

The answer is to do something different. Do something that works. Do something that engages customers and allows the sales call to focus only on what is important to them.

What if you only shared the specific attributes about your product that you knew would be appreciated by your prospect? When great salespeople present, they make it sound like their product was invented for this one specific prospect.

There is only one way to do this: Ask questions!

In order to differentiate yourself, you must make a habit of getting more information than you are giving. You must uncover the emotional, compelling reasons to buy for this one unique prospect. Sandler calls that "finding pain."

FINDING PAIN

Practically speaking, the most important reason people take action is the desire to eliminate pain. Even something that seems like a purchase out of pleasure (say, a decision to build a new outdoor living area) can be based on pain (*I'm jealous when I see my neighbor having great parties outside*). Your first and most important job is to find out if the prospect has any pain—he may not—and, if he does, figure out how your product or service can help solve his problems.

This sounds like it should be one of the simplest steps of every sales call, but it takes more practice than people imagine. It's true that most sales training teaches you to ask questions in order to qualify the prospect. Unfortunately, this advice typically turns into questions like: "Where would you want the keypads for your alarm?" That doesn't tell you anything about this person's specific pain.

Most salespeople claim to understand how important it is to ask good questions, but somehow most appointments or phone calls involve much more of the salesperson's telling than asking.

What are some of the reasons salespeople don't get the customer to talk more? One reason is that they have learned all they possibly can about their product—and are much more comfortable telling.

THE DUMMY CURVE

When most salespeople start with a company, they may not know everything about the product or service. So, in their first meetings with prospects, they naturally ask questions.

Let's say you're a new salesperson and a prospect says, "Can your product do X, Y or Z?" Maybe you don't know the answer to that question. What are you going to do? If you're smart, you'll say something like, "Is that something that is important to you?" or "How would you use X, Y or Z in your home?"

The truth is, you would ask those questions to buy time and help take the focus away from yourself since you don't know all the answers. But, in reality, you would have been conducting a good sales interview.

Sometimes you will hear salespeople say a new member of the team had "beginner's luck." But it's more likely that luck had nothing to do with the sale. Rather, the new person allowed the customer to talk about what was important and why.

Six months into any sales position, it's a whole different story. Filled to the brim with product and company training, the salesperson now has all the answers! When the customer asks, "Can your product do X, Y or Z?" what does he do? If he's like most of us, he starts to spill everything he knows! He not only tells the prospect about X, Y and Z, but also gives a hundred other reasons his product is superior.

At Sandler, we call this the "Dummy Curve." When you're brand new, all you have are questions because you don't know anything about your product or service. You make a bunch of sales anyway. Then some time goes by. You reach the amateur phase, which is where you do know everything about your product or service and mistakenly overshare information. Sales drop. The goal is to become a professional. At that point, you know everything there is to know about your product or service, but you also know that asking questions is more important than spewing information. Sales revive again.

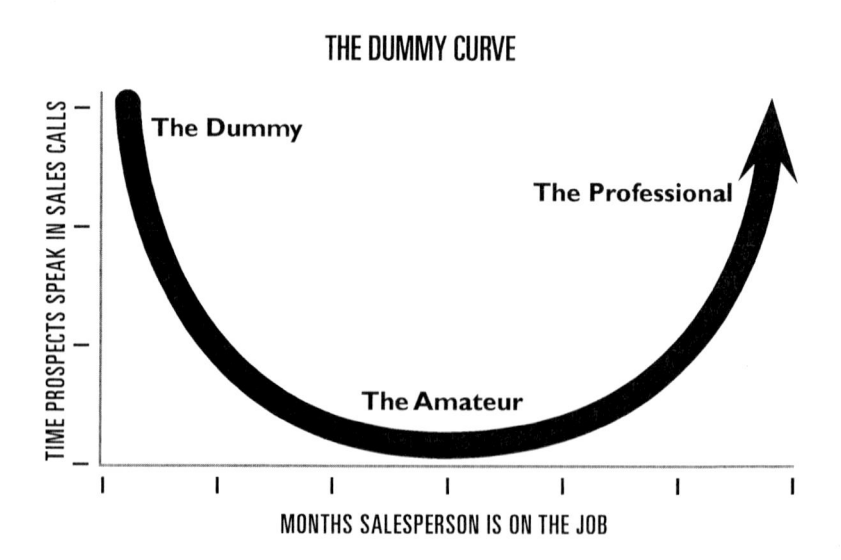

THE DUMMY CURVE

(Y-axis: TIME PROSPECTS SPEAK IN SALES CALLS; X-axis: MONTHS SALESPERSON IS ON THE JOB. Curve shows "The Dummy" at top-left, descending to "The Amateur" at the bottom, then rising to "The Professional" at top-right.)

The more you know, the worse off you are if you cannot wait to share everything you know with the prospect.

The Sandler-trained professional knows that you should learn all you can about your product or service, but learning it and knowing when to share it with the prospect are two different things.

> **SANDLER RULE**
>
> *You should talk 30% of the time on a sales call. The prospect should talk 70% of the time.*

UNDER PRESSURE

Another reason salespeople don't listen to prospects enough is that it's easy to talk too much when the pressure is on.

It is human nature to compensate when you're in a stressful situation, and most salespeople do feel pressure when they are on a sales call with a prospect. But if they don't have a system, that means they usually are "winging it"—letting the customer lead. This provides a perfect storm for more talking than is good for the sales process.

Salespeople who do not follow a system and have not practiced asking the right questions will typically fall into a trap: the minute they hear something positive, they start talking. Here are some examples of questions that cause salespeople to start talking:

Prospect asks: "How soon could you get this installed?"

Prospect asks: "Does your installation come with a warranty?"

This can happen even when salespeople hear something that initially sounds negative:

Prospect says: "That sounds expensive."

Prospect says: "We are looking at a couple of companies before making a decision."

After each of these, most salespeople give an entire monologue of information designed to "sell" the customer. It sounds silly, but it's true. When presented with any kind of stressful situation, even one caused by a "buying signal," many salespeople will respond by talking. And talking. And talking.

A CHANCE TO SHOW OFF

When a prospect mentions something a salesperson knows for sure that his product/service will fix, he wants to jump on it.

Let's say, for example, that a customer mentions he would like to see who comes to the door before he opens it. The salesperson is eager to talk about the different surveillance options that will allow this functionality. Typically, he won't ask about the underlying reasons for the request or why the customer may be concerned about surveillance in the first place. As a result, he misses the opportunity to understand the impact from the customer's perspective if nothing changes. There is no forward motion in the sales discussion.

> **SANDLER RULE**
>
> *Prospects buy for their reasons,*
> *not the salesperson's reasons.*

WHY WE HAVE TO MAKE IT EASY FOR PROSPECTS TO TALK

Which are people more likely to believe: what a salesperson tells them, or what they already believe about their problem?

Allowing the customer to talk more not only gives you critical information about how the prospect sees your product or service, but also automatically gives you more credibility and differentiates you from your competitors. For example, assume the customer explains that the A/C system cools the entire house except for one room, which seems to stay very warm all day long no matter how low he turns the thermostat. This is not the time to say, "Oh, I understand. We can help you with that." A professional salesperson would ask several more questions to further understand the problem and keep the prospect talking.

The Sandler Pain Funnel® questions are designed to help you get information that goes beyond the common or surface reasons for which people say they want to buy. Those "surface problems" are the ones homeowners are likely to share with anyone, including other potential vendors.

Pain Funnel questions, on the other hand, go like this:

"Tell me more about…"

"Give me an example. Can you be more specific?"

"How have you tried to fix the situation before calling us?"

"How did that solution work?"

"How much do you think that is costing you [in time, money, frustration]?"

"How do you feel about that impact?"

"Is this important enough to take care of now?"

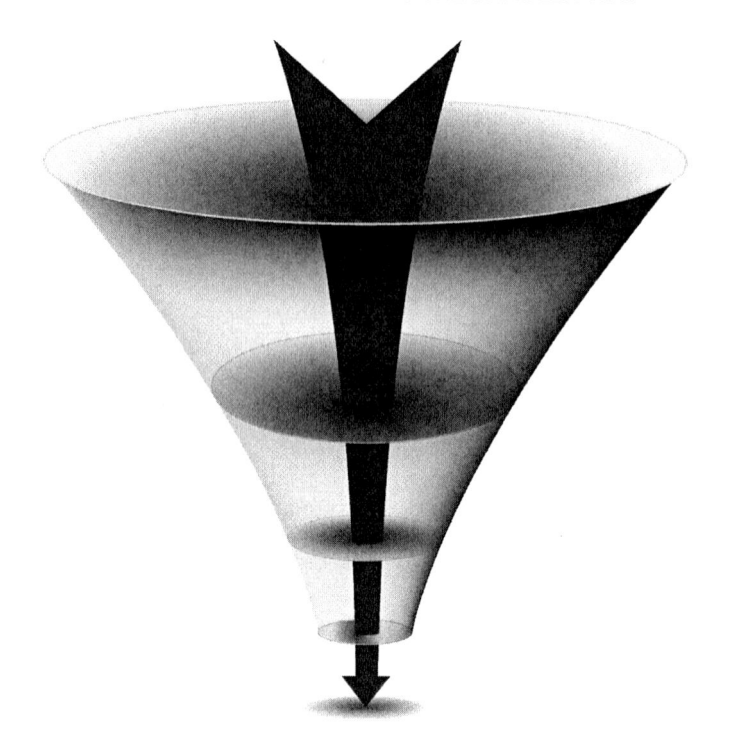

Remember, you want to understand not just the initial problem that the prospect mentions, but the underlying reason for fixing the problem. You want to know how long this issue has been a concern; what other things the prospect has researched to fix the problem; how much the current situation is costing him; what the personal impact of that is; and what happens if the prospect doesn't do anything differently. This process simply lets the customer buy. Most people prefer that over being sold.

A VISIT TO THE DOCTOR

Suppose you go in to see your doctor. You tell her that you have a terrible headache. What if she said:

"Oh, we see that often. We have a great new procedure that

will eliminate your headache. We simply cut through your skull, see what might be causing the pain, remove what we can, and sew you back up. We hope. We have some great prescriptions for you to follow as well. The pharmaceutical company guarantees that you will walk around in a fog for a few days and be unable to work. But your headache might be alleviated if you take the pills. When do you want to schedule the surgery?"

Some doctor! She assumed that you want the surgery. She never asked for an example of what "terrible" might mean to you. She didn't ask how long you had had the pain; what else you had done or taken to get rid of the headache; or what the impact of the headache had been on you, your family or your lifestyle. She asked no questions about other possibly related symptoms either. Most important, there was no discussion of whether you were ready to take the crazy risk of letting her cut your head open.

Believe it or not, that is what happens on many sales calls. A couple calls you into their home; you may ask a few questions (or not), and then you immediately make a bunch of instant assumptions and tell the customers why they should buy your product/service. To continue with the doctor analogy, you are ready to operate. The customers are thinking, *Whoa! Maybe we should just take an aspirin!*

Maybe it's even worse. Maybe you were selling a prospect on fixing a headache and he had a more urgent problem you could solve—but you never asked about other symptoms. You talked and talked and talked and lost his confidence. As a result, someone may come in behind you and get the sale simply because he was able to identify and solve the problem that was important to the customer. You could have solved it, maybe even better, but you were so busy talking you never let the customer share his pain.

Don't let this be you.

BE A DETECTIVE

Detectives are great role models for salespeople.

Whenever a detective is feeling pressure, whether it's because he is concerned about a crime that has happened or is attempting to prevent one from happening, what does he do? He asks questions. Lots of them!

Detectives want to know everything. Their job is to collect information, quickly and accurately, and to look for clues that relate to means, motive or opportunity. Have you ever noticed what happens on TV if a witness starts asking the detective a bunch of questions? The detective asks why the person is so curious!

"Why do you ask?"

"Did you know the victim?"

"Did you see something?"

"Why were you at the crime scene at all?"

You know what detectives don't spend a lot of time doing? Answering questions.

Until they solve the mystery, detectives know they are under no obligation to share everything they know. They must remain unbiased during the investigation phase and figure out who committed the crime.

In classic TV detective shows, sometimes in response to the detective's question, the suspect actually confesses to a crime without being aware that he has shared more information than he intended. Something very similar happens with prospects (though of course you're not out to send them to jail).

Salespeople need to think of themselves as detectives. The job is to find out what is important to prospects and why. You do that by asking questions. The more they talk, the more they may talk themselves into why they want to fix their problem (pain)—and why they want to do it now.

PROBLEMS VS. FEATURES

> **SANDLER RULE**
>
> *Stop selling features and benefits.*

What's the difference between a feature and a problem (i.e., the prospect's pain)? One of the best ways to get clear on the distinction is to understand why people buy from you. What problem do you solve, and how could you describe that problem with an emotional word?

Here are some examples.

Feature: "We have good service."

Problem you solve incorporating an emotional word: "Other customers have come to us because they were *frustrated* with the response time of their prior vendor when they had a question or concern. Is this important to you?"

Feature: "Our product has a lifetime warranty."

Problem you solve, incorporating an emotional word: "Some customers who chose this product were *worried* about buying another product that had no guarantee. Have you ever had an experience with a product that didn't hold up?"

Features are typically listed on marketing materials. But if you think about your own buying habits, you'll realize you don't buy a feature. You buy based on the way you expect that product or service to solve a problem. You may buy a product that has many features, but there are usually one or two specific problems you want to solve. The possibility of solving those problems helps you move forward on the buying decision.

Emotional words and stories about why others decided to work with your company allow you to engage the customer. Share some of the most common reasons other customers come to you and then turn these into a question. Then let the customer talk.

WHY THIRD-PARTY STORIES WORK

There are at least five reasons that stories about other customers are effective:

1. People don't want to be told what to do (or buy, or think). Stories let them draw their own conclusions.
2. You are sharing a story, not convincing anyone of anything.
3. Someone else bought what you sell, making it more OK for this person to consider buying, too.
4. The story validates your experience with specific problems.
5. You can always end with asking the customer a question, which keeps you from making assumptions.

Here is an example of how that approach might be used on the previous alarm call to generate interest and engagement:

"Some of the reasons others in the neighborhood have chosen Super Security Systems to protect their family and property are:

- "They were worried about making sure their home was secure even when they are gone.
- "They are tired of paying for an alarm service that fails to call when the alarm goes off and not getting the responsiveness they were promised.
- "Many parents are concerned about their children opening the door for a stranger because they can't see outside.

"Are any of these important to you?" (Then you can ask Pain Funnel questions!)

Notice that none of these statements talked about how great the product or service was or how long the company has been in business. This is a very different approach than what salespeople typically do. It allows you to appeal to the most likely emotional reasons for someone wanting your product or service.

Also note the importance of asking specific questions. The example didn't say: "What are your top three concerns when it comes to a home alarm system?" If the prospect can even think of an answer, he might say, "Prevention, fast response and dealing with false alarms." The salesperson then says, "Well, you are talking to the right company because we can address all of those." Cue the "talk, talk, talk" machine! In fact, this prospect has shared these exact same concerns with four other alarm salespeople today, and they all said the same thing. The prospect has a feeling of déjà vu.

Good salespeople are happy to let the prospect share their reasons for buying, but they don't stop there. They ask other questions that the prospect had not even considered. For instance:

"Have there been robberies in the neighborhood?"

"Did they occur during the day when the residents were gone or at night when they were there?"

"Are you more concerned about property being stolen?"

"Have you considered where a burglar might try to enter your home?"

"Do you have children or friends that might accidentally set the alarm off?"

All of these questions show a genuine interest in the prospect and further qualify the prospect's willingness to buy. Most importantly, these questions differentiate the salesperson from the other four vendors that the prospect has seen today. Yes, price may still be important to some buyers. It's the salesperson's responsibility to understand what the prospect is prepared or expects to pay. But prospects with more pain are always willing to pay more. In fact, they want to pay more for added services or products. If you encounter a homeowner with a lot of pain, you may actually lose the sale if you do not offer a solution that is more expensive than the competition's. You need the higher price to completely cover the prospect's perception of the problem.

> **SANDLER RULE**
> *If the competition is doing it, stop doing it right away.*

DO SOMETHING ELSE!

Review the features you typically discuss in your own business. Then, convert them to a problem you solve coupled with one of the emotional words below:

Worried	Struggling
Disturbed	Angry
Surprised	Excited
Concerned	Tired of
Overwhelmed	Scared
Frustrated	Upset

Here's an example of how it works.

An outdoor living company offers special equipment to create fine detail and a precise look that maintains architectural integrity. Consequently, the homeowner avoids problems with the local homeowners association or historical society that might otherwise balk at a proposed remodeling project.

Feature: Special equipment able to replicate fine detail

Benefit: Maintain architectural integrity

Problems solved: Fines or complaints by the homeowners association or delays and declines from the local municipalities

Question asked by the salesperson: "Are you concerned about homeowners association rules requiring you to maintain a certain look or architectural requirements?"

Here's another example.

A remodeler uses sophisticated software to predict and

accurately manage how long a certain remodeling job will take and forecast precisely when it will be done.

Feature: Special software and project management capabilities to manage time to completion

Benefit: Job done on time or if problems are uncovered, a new compressed time line is identified

Problems solved: A specific looming deadline creating serious financial and logistical impacts if there are unexpected delays

Question asked by the salesperson: "Are there any specific deadlines that cannot be missed? Are there any aspects of the demolition or the project that might cause delays that you are specifically worried about?"

TWO QUESTIONS

You can often tell immediately whether you have a good chance on a sales call by asking yourself these two questions:

1. "Did I follow the 70/30 Rule?" (If you didn't, you're probably done.)
2. "Did I find any pain?" (No pain, no sale!)

Talking less works because it's the best way to find pain.

Decide today that you are going to talk less, focus on problem identification based on what the customer needs and ask more in-depth questions from the Pain Funnel. If you do that, you will:

- Experience less stress and pressure during the sales call. (After you learn to ask questions you can focus on what

Could Asking Questions Be the Answer?

the customer is saying and not worry about what you are going to say next.)
- Stand out from the competition.
- Qualify or disqualify prospects sooner, rather than later. (Remember, no pain means no sale. You can identify the price shoppers and tire kickers early in the process.)
- Earn more money. (By finding out what is important to the customer, improving your qualifying efforts and reducing stress/pressure in the sales call, you will close more sales.)

Perhaps you've read some of the questions in this chapter and thought, *Oh my, I could never ask that! That's none of my business.* The problem is rarely in the question itself. It's usually how you are imagining the question will sound. If you feel a negative reaction to any questions or examples in this book, we suggest you think about different ways to use tonality to ask the same question. For instance, consider the question, "What are you eating?" If you put the emphasis on each of the four words in turn, you will hear that you are communicating a different message each time.

By the way, this is why we encourage salespeople to interact directly with the customers either in person or "live" on the phone. If you only communicate electronically, you lose the tone and inflection, which can be even more important than the actual words. Prospects will try to get you to communicate over email, but this is less effective than in person or on the phone given your lack of control over the tone and inflection.

QUESTIONS MAKE ALL THE DIFFERENCE

Look at everything our alarm sales professional might uncover using the Sandler Pain Funnel.

Salesperson: "Tell me, what made you decide to look into a new security system for your family?"

Homeowner: "I am a little concerned with some things I have seen on the news. There have been a few burglaries in the surrounding areas."

Salesperson: "Give me an example."

Homeowner: "Well, just some property theft, but they are becoming more frequent."

Salesperson: "How many have you heard about? One or two?"

Homeowner: "No. Probably three or four this year. One in the neighborhood around the corner."

Salesperson: "Oh no, what happened?"

Homeowner: "Fortunately they broke in during the day when both residents were working, but they stole appliances, a little money and tore the place up pretty badly."

Salesperson: "That's awful. Do you know the homeowners?"

Homeowner: "A little. They seemed really upset."

Salesperson: "I'll bet. Were they upset about the home being torn up or the lost appliances?"

Homeowner: "Actually, I think they were more freaked

out about the loss of their privacy. A stranger being in their home. They have insurance so it's not about the money."

Salesperson: "Have you looked into anything else to ease your concerns?"

Homeowner: "Well, we have an old system that is not monitored and can't be upgraded. Then, of course I have a gun and Old Yeller over there."

Salesperson: "How do you think those solutions would protect you and your family if someone tried to break in?"

Homeowner: "The alarm doesn't really work, and the gun is locked up. Old Yeller would just sleep through it."

Salesperson: "Do you suspect they are targeting homes that don't have alarm systems?"

Homeowner: "Yes. I am more afraid if we were here than if we were gone. You never know what can happen these days."

Salesperson: "How are you two feeling about all of this?"

Homeowner: "Sleep isn't what it used to be." (Chuckle.)

Salesperson: "Have you decided this is important enough to fix, or are you still considering keeping the old alarm system in place?"

Homeowner: "No, I'm hoping you can help me get something that will work."

All of this takes practice. Without practice, the novice salesperson would jump in right after the customer said they were concerned about burglaries. The novice would bring out the options and systems that could address that problems. But, the novice would have missed an opportunity to uncover more of the impact and, ultimately, have less focus on the bottom line price and reducing the number of "think it overs."

WHY ASK QUESTIONS?

Many salespeople misunderstand the purpose or intent of all these questions because they think it is their job to manipulate or convince prospects to purchase. But that is a mistake! Gathering all this information before presenting is for the following purposes:

1. Rather than convincing, questions uncover if the prospect is qualified for a proposal or presentation. No convincing is required. This is a huge time-saving technique.
2. When prospects talk about their problems and compelling reasons to buy, they actually convince themselves. Motivational interviewing, appreciative inquiry and several coaching models explain that when subjects (or, in this case, prospects) talk through their situation and state compelling reasons to act, they convince themselves and are statistically more likely to take action.
3. The prospect will build a closer, more trusting relationship with a salesperson who is more concerned about the prospect and determining if he should buy, than with a salesperson who seems not to have the prospect's best interests in mind.
4. Prospects are more likely to think of previously unknown problems when you ask specific questions. They may remember other important problems that they had never considered.

Asking questions like, "Why don't you like your windows?" or "When it comes to windows, what are your top three challenges or concerns?" are alright, but they won't uncover problems the prospect wasn't already considering.

GOOD QUESTIONS CAN BE OPEN OR CLOSED

There is a common misconception by salespeople that they should only ask open questions. (For instance: "How do you and your wife feel about so-and-so?") This misperception occurs because salespeople know that an open question will encourage the prospect to talk more. That is true. But there is still a place for closed questions (otherwise known as "yes or no" questions) that are diagnostic. You can always follow up any closed question with more open questions.

"Does the road noise at night make it harder to sleep?" is a diagnostic question to bring up a specific issue (pain) that homeowners may not have considered because not all homeowners know that soundproofing and windows are related. If the homeowner says, "Yes," you can follow with, "How frequently?" or "What do you do to deal with it?" or simply, "How loud is it?" Closed questions are especially useful when your product or service addresses problems that may differentiate you from the competition. By diagnosing prospects' concerns, you show you care about their situation and you'll be better prepared to make an effective presentation later.

"Do you have a hard deadline by which this project needs to be completed?" is an important closed question that most in-home selling professionals should ask. If the homeowner says, "As a matter of fact we do," it is natural and effective to ask further open questions to understand the deadline and why it is important to the homeowner. The key is to remember to follow each closed question with open questions to keep the prospect talking 70% of the time.

Remember: You're a detective! Be that detective investigating the scene, consumed with what happened or may happen in the future. Get the facts. Learn about people's motives and opportunities. Remain unbiased towards any one individual until you have formulated good proof for your theory.

Give up on trying to convince people. At Sandler, we have worked with thousands of salespeople who now say, "I don't sell. I don't see my job as trying to convince. I'm evaluating prospects' concerns with the intent of identifying if they have any needs that I can fulfill." These same people are doing a good job getting revenue for their company and making a good living for themselves. If you can accept that selling isn't about convincing, you will experience a profound shift in how your conversations develop with prospects. You will sell significantly more even if you don't read the remainder of this book (but please do!).

BE INTERESTED

Interested salespeople are interesting to prospects.

One of the greatest skills that allows salespeople to ask better questions is being able to focus on listening. The discussion should be improvisational, but that doesn't mean it should be unstructured or chaotic.

Did you know that professional improv comedians have rules and tactics they use to hone their craft? Most people think improvisation is a talent that people are born with, that you just have to be quick on your feet. But if you take an improv class, the first thing they will teach you is to focus on what your scene partner is saying. Rather than telling you to think about how you will respond, you'll be encouraged to listen first, think second. That's the source of the scene's structure.

Selling is the same way. Be interested in your prospects. Listen to what they are telling you. Their answers will give you ample cause for more questions.

For example, if you are representing a company that provides a product delivering energy efficiency for the home, you want to find out:

Salesperson: "How much do you think you have spent on your electric bill over the last five years?"

Homeowner: "A lot!"

Salesperson: "I see. In round numbers, what is a lot?"

Homeowner: "Oh, roughly $600 a month. Probably over $30,000."

Note that the salesperson hung in there and got an answer. He made it through the static.

Don't worry about what your next question will be. It's best to practice at the office with your co-workers or trainer. Once you're in a prospect's home, you really should be focusing on listening.

KEY TAKEAWAYS:

- The more prospects talk, the more likely they will buy. The prospect should talk 70% of the time.
- Remember the Dummy Curve: Know all you can about

your product or service, but know when (and when not) to use it.
- Know how to ask all the questions of the Pain Funnel (surface, reasons, impact).
- Use third-party examples based on problems you solve to uncover pain, along with emotional words and questions.
- No pain, no sale!

The fact that prospects have pain does not mean it's time to present a solution. You need to ask even more questions to determine that they are willing and able to buy. You must resist the temptation to present solutions prematurely. In the next chapter, you'll learn why.

CHAPTER FIVE

Are They Willing and Able?

Not everyone who has pain becomes a customer.

John, a sales representative for a landscaping company, meets with a husband and wife at home. John spends about an hour and walks around the outside of the home with the couple.

The three of them discuss what types of plants the homeowners might like; what has and has not done well in this type of soil; and why they want to make their yard more attractive. John finds out that the couple is having a graduation party for their son, a high school senior, and that they are inviting neighbors and family to the event. It will take place in two months. The couple wants their backyard to be beautiful and to require as little maintenance as possible for the rest of the season. When John asks more questions, he finds these prospects have a lot of pain built up around the fact that, right now, they would be embarrassed to have a party in their backyard, and they are feeling overwhelmed given all the other priorities in their lives. They need a company that can take care of everything.

John and the couple get along great during this meeting. The next step is for him to come back in two weeks to review the plan in person. As we hope you've gathered by now, it's best for John to show up in person to go over that plan, not email it. But even that doesn't guarantee a closed sale.

Two weeks later, John comes in and spends about thirty minutes going over the proposed design. He pulls out his tablet computer and shows the homeowners a great presentation that details exactly how the yard will look. He is proud of this proposal. He spent about three hours putting all the options together for the presentation. All that hard work seems to be paying off. The prospects are excited. They're all smiles as he shows them the beautiful designs. They seem to be giving John nothing but buying signals, and they keep saying that they like what they see.

Then John gets to the last page of the presentation.

That's the page that shows the "total investment" of $12,195.

It's like the couple turn into different people. The body language instantly changes for the worse. John sees them trade nervous glances with each other. Their eyes communicate clearly what they don't say out loud: Twelve thousand dollars is way more than they ever thought landscaping could cost.

Nervously, they tell him they will need to think about it. They give him plenty of praise for putting together a top-notch presentation. They tell him how much they appreciate all the hard work he has put in thus far. They tell him they are sure his company would do a great job, but they still need to review their budget for graduation and for all the other things coming up that summer. Their boy is headed for college, after all.

John is terrified he's about to lose what had seemed like a sure thing, so he immediately tells the couple that he could make some changes or maybe even talk to his boss about giving a discount—if they sign today.

This doesn't go over well. They say firmly that they need to think it over.

John is (literally) sweating now. He tells them he understands if they have a problem with the price tag. What if they just pay 30% down, 50% next month, and the final amount two weeks after installation?

This suggestion delivers only more tense facial expressions and more silence. It's too late. The couple is uncomfortable. The husband politely asks John to check back next week, but he's not really asking. He's telling. With no other options, John leaves.

When John checks back the next week, he gets only voicemail. He leaves messages. The messages aren't returned. The couple has gone into that homeowner's equivalent of the witness protection program. They are safe in the final step of the buyer's system. They are hiding.

Possibly something like this has happened to you at some point. Everything is going well, or at least seems to be, right up until the point where the price is discussed. Typically, that is at the end of the proposal/presentation. Then all the work you've done up to that point seems to evaporate. All the goodwill you've built up with the prospect disappears. The prospect needs to think about things. Forever.

Most in-home selling appointments go wrong because price is

only discussed during the final five minutes of the meeting (or, worse yet, in an email message). In this chapter, you will learn to navigate the Budget and Decision compartments of the Sandler Submarine, face-to-face in the first meeting (not the second), with no pressure on either side. We'll also examine some of the reasons in-home salespeople are hesitant to talk about money (a condition known as "head trash," see below) and examine the Sandler response to such issues. We'll also look at how to handle situations where you only have one of two decision makers on hand. Last but not least, we will teach you how to help your "inside coach" (usually one of the spouses) sell to the other decision maker.

WILLING AND ABLE

Buyer behavior is predictable. One behavior that's particularly predictable is that people don't buy if they aren't willing or able to make the necessary sacrifices that will cause the pain to go away. It is the salesperson's job to uncover barriers to a sale prior to presenting, even though the pain is already clear.

Of course, lack of money is a big obstacle—one that can quickly erase any possibility of a sale. It's one of the most common obstacles. The odds of closing the sale go down dramatically when people don't have the money to pay for the product or service.

Unfortunately, often salespeople who uncover what seem like compelling reasons for the prospect to buy (pain) feel a strong desire to present a solution before they've figured out whether or not the prospect is willing and able to buy. That's a big mistake.

Giving a premature presentation kills your closing ratios. Your choice to present should be based on your discussion about the prospect's willingness and ability to make an investment and a decision. Remember the Buyer-Seller Dance. Homeowners expect you to present quickly, like all your competitors do.

But do you have to do it that way, too? Salespeople often deal with prospects who want a premature presentation. It's only natural, so don't worry about it. Remember that you don't have to present until you are ready. After you understand the prospects' pain, the next steps are to find out about their budget and their decision-making process.

We know of a salesperson who sold replacement windows. On one particular call, the salesperson had done a good job of finding many compelling reasons why the homeowner should replace or repair every single window in his home. Some windows couldn't even be opened, the entire family's ability to sleep was affected by the noise of traffic coming through the windows at night and there were even some windows that leaked when it rained. The family had ample compelling reasons to do something about their windows.

However, this homeowner was on a tight budget. He simply didn't have enough money available in his checking account to do all the work at the same time. If this appointment had been handled properly, he might have become a repeat customer over the next five years. Phasing the work would be crucial to closing the sale. If you were to look out one of the windows into the old established neighborhood, you would have seen dozens of homes with the same decrepit windows. The neighborhood was a gold mine. If the salesperson could get one small sale from this homeowner on a tight budget, then every other home was a viable target. Unfortunately, he lost the opportunity by trying to close all the windows in the whole house at once. If he had talked about what the prospect could afford to fix, he'd have been in a much better position.

What salespeople tend to forget is that the Budget Step of the selling system has nothing to do with what they think the project will cost. It's all about what the homeowner is willing and able to spend.

BUDGET TECHNIQUES

Why are salespeople so reluctant to discuss money before presenting? Typically they have been taught to gather information so they can put together the proposal or move to the presentation. If you do a good enough job during those steps, the money will work itself out, right? Wrong.

Salespeople have not been taught why it is important to deal with money early in the process and how to do it in a way that is non-threatening and effective. Once you realize how easy it makes the rest of the sales process and how it helps you determine sooner who is a "suspect" and who is a real prospect, this will become second nature.

Here are some ways to make the Budget Step easier:

1. **Ask if the prospect has done any similar work in the past.** If so, how much did he spend? If he has experience with a similar past purchase, he will have certain expectations and budgets already in his mind.

   "Sally, have you used a pest removal service before?"

   "No, we never have had to."

   In this case the prospect had no previous experience; move on to technique #2.

2. **Use a third-party story.** This works well in many parts of the sale, but can be often used in the Budget Step. You are sharing what other customers have found valuable for them. Here is an example:

    "Other customers like you who have been concerned about keeping bugs out of their home and away from their children usually go with a total maintenance package, which runs about $125 per month. It covers everything and has a complete satisfaction guarantee. Help me understand—is that within the budget that you and Jim have in mind?"

3. **Use words that make people comfortable.**

    "Share"

    "Would you *share* with me what you could set aside to solve this problem?" From childhood everyone is taught sharing is a good thing. "Give" is not as good, especially when you don't know someone well. It is like you are taking something. Many times, salespeople will say: "Can you give me a budget?" Or, "What can you afford?" People may take that as an insult. They can afford a lot of things; it is many times a matter of whether they are going to give something else up.

    "Round numbers"

    People don't want you to reach into their account and get an exact number. But, when you say "round numbers," it softens the discussion. "Would you mind sharing in *round numbers* about what you have set aside for this project?"

4. **Combine both the third-party, round numbers and sharing.**

    "Polly, *other customers* have found it valuable to *share* with us a budget that is important to stay within as we develop a proposal for their new outdoor living space. Some will give us a range that is comfortable for them. Would you help me understand, in *round numbers*, what works for you?"

5. **Bracket.** Some customers have no idea what your product or service costs or what it takes to solve the problems (pain) you have uncovered before discussing budget. Many salespeople offer levels of solutions based on what the prospect can afford. Offering a range or bracket can help you understand what they are willing (and able) to invest. Kind of "good, better and best."

"Mrs. Smith, we can help you solve the problems we discussed and get your kitchen up-to-date. In order to make sure we respect and stay within the budget you have in mind, help me understand what would be best for you. The high-end appliances and top-of-the-line materials for this project might be $35,000–$45000; a mid-level selection would be $25,000–$35,000; or we could address the most urgent areas to get the kitchen functional for around $10,000–$15,000. What are you thinking would work for you?"

THE "SNAP JUDGMENT" BUDGET ISSUE

It's tempting on your drive through the neighborhood to make judgments about how much a homeowner can spend before you even speak to him. That is a mistake! Just because the homes appear expensive or the cars in the driveway are brand new doesn't mean your specific prospect can or wants to spend the money necessary to pay for your product or service. Some people spend very little on vehicles and choose to spend those savings on their home. Others spend money on fancy cars and jewelry and have very little left over after paying their mortgage. We've stressed the importance of using a system for selling. Part of the effectiveness of this system is it will keep you from wasting time with prospects who aren't willing and able to spend on your product or service. You will also be able to identify and close sales that other salespeople didn't take seriously. Use the system with every prospect. Avoid the temptation to make judgments about people's finances.

> **SANDLER RULE**
> *Never look in your prospect's pocket.*

HEAD TRASH, MONEY AND AUTHORITY

The authors of this book were each raised in families where one was taught never to speak to strangers about money.

You would never ask someone what he made in salary or what he paid for something. You definitely would never talk to family members or close friends about income or what they paid for that new car in the garage or their new country club membership or the beautiful oil on canvas from the unpronounceable artist they proudly display in their living room. In fact, come to think of it, you probably shouldn't talk about financial matters, period!

The widespread discomfort about discussing money is almost laughable—but there's nothing funny about it. It is a real impediment to success for salespeople. After all, your job is to discuss money, budgets, investments, return on investment and even the source of the prospect's money. So this is a piece of "head trash" (thought patterns and tendencies that keep you from responding professionally) you have to discard.

THE AUTHORITY ISSUE

Recently, we were training a client on questioning techniques. He was learning to ask pain questions. Instead of jumping in and answering the question, the salesperson would make sure to understand the "if and why" of what is important to the prospect. So, our client asked another question back to the prospect. We role-played, and he seemed to be learning quickly. As we wrapped up the training session, he went back to working the phones. Shortly afterwards, we overheard him using some of the techniques exactly as we had practiced. He closed a sale that had been in the works for some time. Victory, right? Then he picked up an incoming call. His tone changed completely. It was as if he had never heard of Sandler, much less learned any techniques about asking questions. In this second conversation, he caved. He had completely regressed in a snap.

All this client's incoming calls are recorded with the caller's knowledge, so we were able to listen to the call later. We were curious to learn whether there was something unusual about the call. It sounded like a normal call to us: A middle-aged man called to inquire about the products this company sold with the standard questions. Nothing out of the ordinary, at least to our ears. We played the call for some others at the company, though, and they immediately noted what we had missed.

This particular prospect spoke with a very authoritarian tone. He sounded intimidating to the salesperson we had trained. Previously when the salesperson had been using the techniques successfully, he had been speaking to a soft-spoken prospect. Apparently that caller wasn't intimidating to him.

Sometimes salespeople have a challenge speaking to people they perceive to be of higher authority. These prospects may not have a name tag or title that gives them formal authority—they may just sound or look intimidating.

Some prospects make strong attempts to assert their authority so as not to be taken advantage of by traditional salespeople. In the previous example, the salesperson heard a voice that triggered deep memories of interactions with authority figures, and he immediately regressed to being that 7-year-old who was instructed to do whatever the principal says or suffer extreme consequences. We worked with this salesperson to help him become more comfortable in his role. If we hadn't, he would still be following every order issued by prospects who sound authoritative without asking any questions whatsoever.

In the end, it's a matter of deciding to embrace your role. Salespeople are not the only ones who have to learn how to do this. Police officers and doctors must go through some kind of major transformation in their professions. Initially they are the obedient students willing to work hard for recognition and to obtain their licenses or certifications. Then suddenly they are supposed to be a brand-new person who cannot be intimidated by others, whether they are interacting with an unruly patient or a manipulative swindler. Yes, it is true that prospects can be unruly and even manipulative. It only makes sense that successful salespeople must make a similar transformation to deal effectively with their prospects and learn which of them are willing and able to buy.

THE PAIN/BUDGET SEESAW

You can think of selling as a process to identify the optimum design, product or solution based on balancing the prospect's pain against his willingness and ability to spend. If the prospect has "heavy" pain but a "light" budget, no sale will take place.

WHY HOMEOWNERS REALLY POSTPONE THE SALE

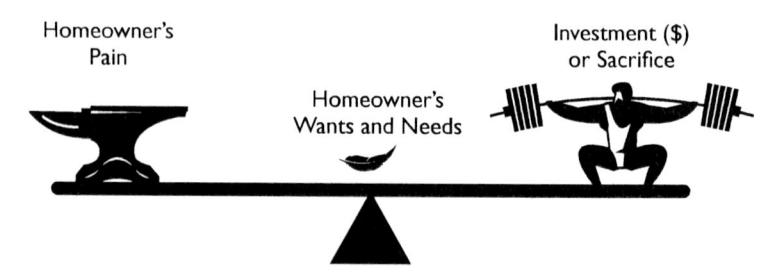

Homeowner's Pain

Investment ($) or Sacrifice

Homeowner's Wants and Needs

Prospects' pain must be greater than their willingness to sacrifice or no sale will take place. Furthermore, prospects act unpredictably when they are asked to sacrifice when there is no pain.

Here's a surprise. If the client is able and willing to spend a "heavy" budget (yes, that does happen from time to time) and the pain you are solving is "light," the seesaw is still out of balance and no sale will take place. Most salespeople think they lose deals if their price is too high. Yet many salespeople lose deals because their price is too low.

You may have heard this before without realizing what was happening: "Thank you for your estimate, Mr. Salesperson. We really appreciate it. It's clear you've put a lot of time into this, and your pricing seems fair to us. However, we aren't sure what we want to do at this time." Or, "This is a very interesting estimate that is very enticing. We want to weigh all our options for now."

The optimum sale is one where the pain and the budget are in balance, like a seesaw or scale where the two sides are level. It's the salesperson's responsibility to uncover information that will help him to understand whether and how it is possible to create this balance.

The entire point of a selling system is to identify information that will allow you to craft a proposal that will win the business—or to allow you to decide that there is no hypothetical proposal that can win the business. Either choice is acceptable. It is the responsibility of the salesperson to decide whether pain and budget are in balance, and whether the prospect is worthy of further consideration by the salesperson.

- If the cost of resolving the pain does not match up with the available budget, then the salesperson must re-engage with the prospect and get a clearer sense of the prospect's priorities before deciding to proceed.
- If the pain and budget seem balanced like the seesaw example, then it's time to proceed.

WILLINGNESS IS NOT ABILITY

At this point you may be thinking, "OK, OK—so I've got the prospect's pain, and I know the prospect has a realistic budget. Let's get on with the presentation already!"

It's a common response. Why should you have to bother getting even more information before presenting? The frustration is understandable, but think of it this way: You have carried the ball to the 10-yard line and you can practically feel a touchdown. Does a professional let his guard down in the last moments? If anything, the professional becomes even more alert the closer he is to success.

Many years ago, author Chip visited the famous Rodeo Drive in Beverly Hills. The streets and building were immaculate, and there were lots of tourists walking around. He took the obligatory pictures and left. He himself never went into any of the stores or shops. Chip has shared this story with hundreds of people, and practically everyone else that has also been there told us the same thing: They didn't go into any of the shops either. There's a simple reason for this inclination. People don't want to be embarrassed by looking at things that they can't afford.

In order to maintain rapport with many of your prospects, you absolutely must ensure you know what they are both willing and able to spend before you present. If you fail to do so, you may very well embarrass your prospect. People don't buy from salespeople who embarrass them.

Perhaps you are thinking that if they can't afford what you sell, then it doesn't matter if you maintain rapport. Actually it does. The prospect may need to be disqualified, but even a bad prospect can be a good referral source. With all the social media sites and online reviews that are crucial to businesses, especially businesses that sell to homeowners, we recommend you do everything possible to avoid embarrassing prospects or telling unqualified prospects how much you charge. They will go online and share their own impressions with the world, even though they did not become a customer. Often the worst reviews are from those homeowners who did not choose to work with the company. This may seem unfair, but as long as it happens, you should take precautions. If you do, you will be less likely to suffer from a disqualified prospect's wrath.

There are four more great reasons to learn about the prospect's willingness and ability to spend:

1. With most in-home sales products, the prospect has an unrealistic budget expectation. This is merely a fact of the industry. It's no reason to be frustrated with homeowners. They just don't know. Some have even spent hundreds of hours watching some cable channel talking about home flipping, costs of improvements and extreme home makeovers that include the price of airfare and a visit to Disneyland. But they still may have unrealistic expectations of what they should pay and how long the work will take. Rather than work up a proposal, it's in your best interests to see how far off you are and then decide if the prospect is worth pursuing.

2. You have some flexibility in what you offer. Sure, you may want to sell the top-of-the-line product, but would you rather try to sell that and risk getting nothing or promote the smaller, more economical sale that will sufficiently meet the customer's needs and turn him into a repeat customer and ongoing referral source to you for life?

3. Estimates and proposals take time. How much do proposals cost your company every year? How much revenue do they actually generate? You should calculate this. Don't imagine the customer never shows your estimates to anyone else. What signals do your estimates and proposals send to your competition?

4. Even if you can print a proposal in a meeting with no hard costs to your company, you lose all your leverage by doing so. After all, that's why the prospect invited you to his

home—to give a proposal. This is unpaid consulting, or "valuable information for free." Once you provide it, you are playing the prospect's game. Expect to be thanked and hurried to the door shortly after you've given the prospect his price, since that is all he wanted in the first place. Your role as salesperson is now finished in his eyes. His eyes are glazed over. Even if you can manage to stay in his living room, his period of engagement is done.

WHAT MAKES IN-HOME SALES DIFFERENT

The prospect's willingness to buy may have nothing to do with his ability to buy.

Think about it. Salespeople who sell to businesses are taught to meet with the economic buyers and other key decision makers. The ability to buy sometimes may even be reflected in a person's particular department or job title. This is not the case with in-home selling. Your prospects may be salivating at the thought of buying your product or service and may be ready to sign today. But that doesn't mean a sale should happen.

It's quite possible there are great reasons not to pursue this deal. Examples may include the prospects' ability to overcome homeowners association or county building codes. They may have good intentions in trying to procure a home equity loan to build an addition or replace their furnace, bathroom or kitchen, but no ability to do so because of credit problems. There are countless variations, of course.

The prospect's willingness and his ability may be worlds apart. In some cases, the only way you can close the sale is by understanding and later facilitating his buying process with the bank, county or homeowners association. We have seen countless situations where, without the salesperson's involvement, no sale would have occurred.

HOMEOWNERS DON'T HAVE A STRUCTURED DECISION-MAKING PROCESS

Another factor in getting decisions is whether the salesperson thinks that whatever decision in question is an easy one. If homeowners have never made a decision to spend six figures on remodeling their home and the salesperson thinks spending six figures is a lot of money, it is highly unlikely that the salesperson will get the homeowners to decide to spend six figures in the first sales call. On the other hand, if all the homeowners have to decide is whether to come to the company's showroom to look at appliances, cabinets and countertops after the first meeting in the home, that is a decision that is much more likely to happen. Both the salesperson and the homeowners feel that is a reasonable decision to make.

You have to provide a process that allows your prospects to make decisions in a safe and intelligent manner. If you have a website with a page titled, "How we work with clients," then you probably already have these steps identified. If you use an automated system for tracking, these steps are often labeled as "stages." Don't use the default stages in your automated system. Create your own that map to how you work with clients.

The key here is that the prospect may have pain and be willing and able to buy, but not have a structured process to ensure he is making the right decision. It is the company's responsibility to provide a safe and low-risk process to homeowners to reassure them that they are making the best choice.

> "Actions speak louder than words—
> but not nearly as often."
> —Mark Twain

You will use up-front contracts to ensure that the prospects make decisions and take actions that move in an orderly fashion through each stage of your sales process. Your competitors may say things like, "What will it take to earn your business?" or "We are prepared to offer you a special price, but it will expire tomorrow." Instead, you will allow your clients to make decisions on incremental actions. Having a process for the customer to follow will put you far ahead of your less-sophisticated competitors. When the prospects feel they are in control, making intelligent low-risk decisions and investing more time and energy with your company at every step, they are much more likely to buy in the end. Their actions to visit your showroom, pay for a small design agreement or do whatever else you request is very indicative of their intent to buy. Most importantly, they will feel it was their own idea to select your company.

From the earlier example, Kathy, the inside salesperson with Perfectly Posh Pools, ensured the prospect agreed to make a decision about a design. If your inside salesperson is incapable of discussing these up-front contracts on the phone, then the salesperson should do so when calling to confirm the appointment. Because homeowners don't have a structured process, it is crucial that they understand the decisions about next steps, such as a service charge for an appointment, paying for a design, a visit to the showroom or a deposit to order equipment.

WHO'S THE DECISION MAKER?

When you talk to a homeowner, how do you know you are talking to the final decision maker? Sometimes it's hard to tell. Real estate agents may be involved in window decisions. Bankers could be involved in kitchen remodeling decisions. Financial advisors or estate planning attorneys might be involved in decisions about house additions. It's complex!

Of course, the classic issue that all in-home sellers eventually run into is the involvement of the spouse or partner. Some companies—not all—even stereotype and assume non-working spouses may not have the ability to decide on a financial expenditure by themselves. Big mistake!

We're talking about ability to buy. Ability is a more comprehensive topic than, "Mrs. Jones, you will need to ensure Mr. Jones can join us at our meeting." Ouch! We've seen thousands of examples where salespeople make a point of ensuring that all decision makers are there for the discussion—and then destroy any rapport they had built by issuing that one commission-killing instruction.

Rather than viewing ability as a holistic topic that is unique to each home, some salespeople simply insist that the other spouse "must attend." Instead, if they were to approach the ability question as an equation where the spouse is a variable that needs to be solved, they could avoid unnecessary damage to rapport and improve the odds of closing the sale.

THE COUPLE PROBLEM

Husbands and wives. Wives and husbands. Significant others and significant others. How do you get them to arrive at a decision that both will endorse? Here's one approach.

"Pat, most of the time when I work with couples, they make decisions based on different things. As we go through our discussion today and you see something that Brett might want or need more information on, let me know and I can make a note, OK?"

When it comes to in-home selling, you sometimes receive the gift of the "inside coach": the partner in the relationship who is backing you. To get inside coaches, though, you have to set them up to sell for you and you have to find out where the other spouse has pain.

If you're talking to one spouse, you will likely be warned ahead of time that a decision to purchase will not happen until the other spouse is consulted. Here's one good way to respond to that.

"Pat, I know you said you have to run this by Brett. Most couples work together on these decisions. Based on what you have seen and what we discussed about how our garage organization system would help you solve your space problems, I'm curious about something. When you talk to Brett, what are you going to recommend as the next step?"

You'll learn a lot from what happens next. Ideally, what you hear will tell you how this person will sell your product or service to his or her spouse. It's not that the person might have a problem with the purchase. (If there's a problem, you want to know what it is!) It's when the person says something like, "It looks great! I love it!" but doesn't give any reason as to why. Too many salespeople hear that and think, *I've got a closed deal!* Actually, what they've got is a problem with that sales drug "hopium." They hope they've got a deal—but hope does not a closed deal make. The discussion needs to continue until you either identify a problem or you hear the person state the specific reasons why it makes sense to buy. Those are the reasons this person will share with a spouse.

Remember you are often only asking the spouse to make a small decision to go to the next step. (Example: Make an appointment to visit your showroom, pay a smaller amount for a design or simply decide if the couple would like to meet with you again in the future.) This brings us to the next part of the conversation, which might go like this:

> **Salesperson:** "Pat, when you talk to Brett, based on what you have seen, what are you going to recommend as the next step?"
>
> **Pat:** "Oh, I will tell him we should work with you."
>
> **Salesperson:** "OK. How do you think our product will help you the most?"
>
> **Pat:** "I think it will save us so much time searching for things and reduce some of the stress of having the constant clutter."

That is a good answer. But, if you didn't ask about Pat's recommendation on next steps and why, you may not be able to discern whether Pat is just being nice or is actually going to recommend the product. Know before you leave whether you have a champion, why you have a champion and how you can help get to the next step.

Ask inside coaches what they are going to recommend, and then monitor tone, body language and word choice carefully in order to see where you stand. The next time you are getting ready to prepare pricing and share all your expertise, make sure you have discovered the prospects' pain, you have discussed a budget/range and you understand the steps in the decision-making process. You can save both yourself and your prospects time and energy by making sure you stay within the parameters already discussed. This takes the pressure off when it comes to closing the sale for both you and your prospects.

WHAT'S THE TIMELINE?

An important part of evaluating your prospects' willingness and ability to make a decision is the timeframe. If you've already found pain, that means the homeowners have an important problem they want to fix. But when? Now is the time to find out.

Never give a presentation unless you know what will happen next—and when. For most in-home sales, there are three important dates:

1. When the homeowner wants the problem eliminated.
2. When the homeowner wants to start the project.
3. When the homeowner wants to choose a company to do the work or service.

We recommend asking these questions in this particular order. You don't want to sound "sales-y" by starting with, "When will you be picking a company?" In many cases, homeowners will answer question #1 by saying that they want the problem addressed right away, which then makes their answers about when to start and when to select a company much more urgent. Prospects need to think about these three questions in this "reverse order" so that they are more likely to give a realistic and timely answer to the final question.

KEY TAKEAWAYS:

- Prospects must be both willing and able to invest in your product or service.
- Discussing money may not initially be comfortable, but it is part of your job to qualify or disqualify a prospect.
- Don't wait until the end of the presentation to discuss budget. It puts too much pressure on you and the prospect.
- Ask for a decision (a clear next step) on each call.
- It is always best to have a face-to-face meeting with all decision makers; avoid sending a quote without a set time to review with them.
- If you must utilize the "inside coach" strategy, ask whether the one to whom you are speaking would recommend your product or service and why. Then, find out what information the other decision-making partner may need to have.

In the next chapter, you'll learn how to present only what is important to the buyer.

CHAPTER SIX

When in the Customer's House, Let the Customer Buy

> **SANDLER RULE**
>
> *If you wait until the presentation to close the sale, you put too much pressure on the prospect—and yourself.*

A salesperson named Whiff representing a financial services/life insurance company went out on a promising second appointment at the home of a young couple. The husband and wife, in their twenties, had first met Whiff as the result of a referral from another client.

The couple had just bought a new home. They had a young family and wanted to make sure they were adequately insured. Whiff had already had a good first meeting with them, and now he came back to discuss potential solutions to help them meet their financial objectives and protect the family. After some bonding and rapport, the three of them moved to the kitchen table to go over the proposal. It was huge—pages and pages of summaries, spreadsheets and sample policies. Whiff talked and talked for about an hour as the couple obediently nodded their heads from time to time.

After going through the various details of the quotes, Whiff passed along another thick packet that included brochures, illustrations and helpful information on both the company and the representative.

Then he said the phrase that so often causes in-home sales to die a premature death: "Here are all the options I have put together for you. Let me know as you go over this if you have any questions."

Earlier that day, his manager had told him, "You need to make sure you follow up!" So of course, he continued with this guaranteed commission-killer: "I will check in with you later in the week and see if you are ready to get started."

Secure in the knowledge they had given no commitment to make any decision whatsoever, the couple looked everything over, then started the ritual wind-down of the conversation. The right pleasantries about traffic and weather and the journey back to the office were exchanged. The couple thanked Whiff for all of his hard work. Obviously, they said, a lot of time and effort had gone into his proposal. He had given them a lot to think about. (Have you heard this story before?)

So what happened next? You guessed it. The weekend passed. Whiff checked back in. No human being answered the phone. A few more days go by. Whiff left another message. "Hey there, I am just checking in to see if you had a chance to look over those future values for the life insurance. Give me a call at…" Nothing.

By now you know—though maybe Whiff still didn't—that this "good call" wasn't going anywhere. The potential customer has gone into hiding.

At least in this situation, there had been a second appointment face-to-face. What went wrong?

THE "GOOD CALL"

Several things went off track here even before the salesperson presented the quote.

- The salesperson did not set the stage at the beginning of the call as to the potential outcomes of the discussion. In other words, there was no up-front contract.
- The salesperson jumped right from bonding and rapport and into a discussion of the quotes, without getting the couple back into pain. He made no effort to re-engage on the problems they discussed on the first visit. He did not ask if anything had changed or if there were any other issues to cover.
- There was no solid discussion about money or the decision-making process. There was no discussion of the timing for implementation or the timing to make a decision and sign some sort of an agreement.

But even if the salesperson had done all of those things perfectly, there were some other big problems.

- Supposedly, salespeople want to avoid the "think it over" outcome. Yet the salesperson basically told the couple to "think it over" by saying, "Let me know if you have any questions." Of course, they were happy to oblige.
- The salesperson gave the couple way too much information: multiple choices; brochures; packets full of stuff to go through after the meeting. All that does is make customers think: *Wow. We are going to need a lot of time to review all of this. There are a lot of options and a lot of supporting materials to consider.* In fact, many prospects would prefer fewer choices. They may say they want to see all the options, but once those options are presented, they become confused and unsure. Too much information and too many choices can hurt the salesperson's chances for closing a sale.

At this stage in the selling process, your presentation and the prospect's reaction to it should be completely predictable. Theoretically, you should never present unless you know what the prospect will buy and when.

If you get unhooked from "hopium" and uncover all the information in the compartments of the Sandler Submarine, you will see how unsurprising your presentation should turn out to be. You have uncovered the prospects' pain, understood their willingness and ability to spend and learned about their timing and requirements to decide. You should be presenting something that summarizes what the decision makers already know. This is no time to throw in new information to confuse the prospect or complicate the decision.

After that disastrous presentation, in one of his voicemails, Whiff provided a helpful excuse to the customer: "You are probably just busy..." This happens often. Salespeople leave all kinds of lengthy, submissive voicemails or emails—messages that make them seem "less than" to the customer. This is a difficult problem for many sales professionals to overcome, especially if they felt that the prospects liked them and they had a good rapport. That means nothing without a compelling, emotional reason to buy and without having agreed to a clear course of action.

NO BOBBLE-HEAD PRESENTATIONS

Whiff's presentation followed the "bobble-head" approach. The salesperson does most of the talking, throwing in lots of buzz words and industry jargon and numbers. The customers look interested during this monologue (although sometimes, they don't), and they may nod their heads up and down from time to time like a bobble-head doll. But they are not truly engaged if the salesperson is doing all of the talking.

Whiff never asked, "How do you think this would solve your concerns about protecting your family?" He had no real way to gauge whether they would move forward and buy the policy. Additionally, there was no clear next step. The "I'll check in later this week" line was a way to avoid asking whether this was important enough for the couple to take action. Whiff said that for one simple reason: He didn't know what else to say. Salespeople can't close if they don't know what to ask the prospect to do.

If you have worked hard to find a qualified prospect who truly is interested in your product or service, you don't want to get in your own way and spend precious time "checking in," "following up" and not getting messages returned.

Instead, set a strong up-front contract. If this is a typical appointment where you have everything you need to close the sale, consider using what we call the "final up-front contract." This is where you set the expectation that if things go well, that will be the time to write up the order. Or, they should tell you "no" at that stage if this is not the right solution for them. There is no middle ground, no "think it over" option in this up-front contract. It might sound like this:

> "Sam, do we still have about an hour today? Great. We wanted to review the designs and solutions we came up with for your outdoor living area. I'll have some additional questions for you, and you may have thought of some questions or ideas since we last met. Typically, at the end of our meeting today we should both make a decision and decide to work together and get the paperwork started to build your backyard oasis; or, as we discussed before, if we are not the right solution for you, we can choose not to move forward. Sound fair?"

Why are salespeople hesitant to set the stage for a *yes* or *no*? It probably has something to do with being scared of the word "no." That's head trash.

Salespeople believe that the more prospects they have in the pipeline, the better. This makes them look better (they think) to their manager. Even if they have heard, "No, we bought from your competitor," they believe there is still hope. The more invested they are in terms of the time and energy they have put into the

---

SANDLER RULE

You can't lose anything you don't have!

sales process, the more timid some salespeople can be about getting commitment. Don't be one of those.

Remember: People will not decide to say "no" just because you said they could. If they want to buy from you, they will. We have found that salespeople who try to box the prospect in and allow only a *yes* create additional resistance. If prospects feel they can't say "no," they are far more likely to choose that option anyway, or at least say they need more time. Similarly, if prospects feel that *no* is an acceptable option to the salesperson, they are more likely to say "yes." If they have no intention of moving forward, they will be more likely to tell you so if you make it easy for them to say "no." That's important, because you don't want to chase people around and never get a response.

Every time you tell prospects they can say "no," and particularly when you do so before a presentation, you gain instant credibility. You look and act as if you don't need the business. By doing this, you become a consultant who stands out from other salespeople. Good salespeople get decisions. They don't always get a *yes* answer, but they do get a decision. They know that a *no* can be a valuable time saver if it is the right decision for the prospect.

DEFUSE ANY BOMBS EARLY

Sometimes a salesperson gives the entire presentation only to hear from the prospects, "We had some unexpected expenses come up. This is a great proposal, but we probably will not look into doing this project until next year."

It happens all the time. You go on what you think is a closing appointment with all the right forms, a beautiful proposal and the commission already spent on a great vacation. But when you step into the appointment you find:

- The right people are not there.
- You do not have enough time to do a good job getting the prospect back to pain, going over solutions, getting commitment and so forth.
- Something changed. Maybe a competitor came in; maybe there is a money issue; maybe the prospects looked into things on the Internet and now have quite a bit of (mis)information.

All of these are bombs waiting to go off in the middle of your sales process. Follow the below rules to uncover any bombs early.

After the final up-front contract, ask immediately: "Has anything changed since we last spoke/met?" If so, evaluate and adapt.

If you absolutely need all decision makers there and one is missing, explain what's in it for them if they wait until there is time for a good discussion and why you need to reschedule.

For example, if you represent a company that offers independent home-based business opportunities, it may be very important that all decision makers are at your presentation.

"Sally, typically when both spouses can't be here it makes sense to reschedule. Other customers have shared with me that when they are not able to review the program together, learn about why others have seized this opportunity for additional income, and have specific questions from both of them answered, they were not able to evaluate whether this would even be right for them. In order for you and Scott to decide what works best for you, let's invest the time to do this all together and get the information you need."

If someone shopping for a garage door says a competitor has come in and they mention the company name, deal with that directly.

"I understand. I hear Garages 101 is a good company. [Pause.] My job today is to ask you some additional questions about what is important to you. After meeting with them, you may have come up with some additional questions for me. I can share why other customers like you have chosen Super Duper Garages as their vendor. Either way, you will decide if we are the right solution for you."

If they're selling or renting their house and mention they got a lower price/quote, deal with that directly.

"Bob, it makes sense that you want to make sure you are getting the best value. [Pause.] My job today is to review what you and Lisa find most important when selecting a real estate professional. I have some additional questions for you since we last met, and you may have come up with some for me. I can share with you why other clients have chosen my services even though there are lower-price options. Then, you can both decide if I am the right fit for you. If not, that is OK as well."

The point is to be calm, not defensive. For instance, never bash the competition. That only makes customers want to defend the competition, even if they don't particularly like them.

Knowing what is going on early in the call helps you adapt your presentation and questions. In the price example, notice that the above gives the customer a little ego boost: "It makes sense that you want to make sure…" This subtly communicates that you are on his side.

By the way, what is the alternative to what we've outlined? Wait until the last five minutes of the meeting to find out what is really going on? That will only put too much pressure on yourself and the prospect.

DO NOT PRESENT TOO SOON

It's important to have most of the sale and commitment complete before going over the details of any proposal. In the Sandler system, the proposal is called the Fulfillment Step. By this stage, you should only be presenting what is important to this prospect. That should only come after:

- You have uncovered pain (problems that are important to the customer and you know you can solve).
- You know there is a budget and what it is.
- You are in full agreement with the homeowner about what the decision-making process will look like.
- If this is not the first appointment, you have reviewed all of the above with the prospect, the prospect has re-engaged and said what is important to him and he is committed to wanting to make a *yes* or *no* decision on a solution today.

Delaying the presentation is not easy. Salespeople are taught to quote and quote. Throw enough out there, the story goes, and somebody will buy. What this mindset forgets, though, is that people buy in spite of the pitch, not because of it. If you want to close the tough sale, the one that could go either way, the only reliable way to do that is by obtaining all the information up front.

EQUIP YOUR INSIDE COACH

Sometimes, during this meeting, you will not get in front of both people who will impact the decision. If that is the case, you will need to ask two main questions:

> "Carol, based on what we have discussed, what will your recommendation be to Reid about moving forward with our solution?"

Now be quiet! If you hear a favorable response, ask: "Why do you think we are the right company for you?" As you recall from our previous chapter, you want Carol to be able to articulate what is most important to her personally about working with you. If she won't share with you any specifics, she may only be telling you she'll recommend you to be polite.

If all is good on step one and your inside coach is committed to recommending a clear next step and can explain why you are the best solution, then help this person adapt to the other person (the partner), who likely has a different communication pattern and buying style. So for instance, you might say:

> "Carol, many times when I work with couples, each person evaluates things differently. When you talk with Reid, is there any information that he may want to see that you and I have not covered, so I can make sure you have what you need to show him?"

Then you can put together something simple to allow Carol to sell on the points that are most important to Reid. This is a mandatory two-step process that most salespeople miss when they are in a situation where they cannot see all decision makers.

LET THE CUSTOMER BUY

Remember: This is a discussion. You discuss problems, budget, decision making and your best solutions to the problems. If you do all that, you will be likely to set up an agreement that allows the customer to buy—as opposed to you selling. It might sound like this:

> "Kyle, if we can solve the problems you are having with your landscape, stay within the budget we discussed and work with you and Mary to create a timeline that gets your yard ready before you put it on the market, what would be the next step?"

You may be surprised the first time the customer says, "Well, I guess we need to go ahead and get it going." But that's what's going to happen!

Surprise, surprise. You didn't even need a long proposal. You didn't need the pressure of the close. You can just write up the order and get started.

Other simple closes that allow the customer to buy sound like this:

"Is this something important enough to go ahead and fix?"

"What do you see as our next step?"

"Are you ready to solve your concerns about..."

"If nothing changes, what would be the impact..."

"Where do we go from here?"

"On a scale of 1–10, with 1 being you are not at all interested and 10 being you are ready to get this project started today, where are you now?" (If they answer somewhere between 5–9, you can ask, "What would you need to see in order to be at a 10?")

Remember: People do not like to be sold; they like to buy.

Traditional sales techniques focus on pulling the customer toward making a buying decision. Often, this approach backfires. The harder the salesperson pressures the prospect to buy, the more the prospect pulls away—and then the more the salesperson pressures to buy. By using the ideas we have shared in this chapter, you can take the pressure off—and make it easy for homeowners to do the buying.

KEY TAKEAWAYS:

- Do not present before you have covered pain, budget and decision-making authority.
- You must get the prospect back in pain before a presentation at a subsequent meeting.
- Using a strong up-front contract can diffuse any bombs early in the meeting.
- Present only what is important to the prospect (solve his pain).
- Let the customer close the sale: "Based on what you have seen, what do you see as the next step?"

In the next chapter, we will help you prioritize the activities in your day and manage your most valuable resource—time.

CHAPTER SEVEN

Don't Go Broke Being Busy

Sometimes salespeople mistake activity for productivity. Successful salespeople are careful about the commitments they make to prospects.

Danny is a salesperson for Canine Coop, an invisible fence company. He starts his day early, organizing his appointments and calls—including initial contacts with people who have responded to the company's advertising. He also has to call referrals from homeowners, local shelters and veterinary centers that send prospects his way.

Danny's day is full of sales calls, and most of the time he is in a hurry. He barely has time to gather all the information he needs at each location to provide a quote. He is so busy he typically doesn't get home until about six in the evening. Then he grabs a quick bite to eat with his family and works for two more hours on all the proposals and quotes he promised to send out that day. He feels accomplished when he gets everything out on time, and he always tells his boss he has "no shortage of good prospects."

Sounds good, right?

Here is the problem: Danny is on commission, and he's not making enough money to pay his bills.

Canine Coop's owner Bill does not understand why Danny does not close more sales. He is also frustrated that when Danny does close sales, many of them are discounted. This cuts into Bill's income as well.

> *Don't let your pipeline be full and your bank account be empty.*

"Don't let your pipeline be full and your bank account be empty"—that is what's happening with Danny.

A salesperson who is overwhelmed with work but not making money is in big trouble. So is the salesperson on the other end of the spectrum who doesn't have many prospects, but fills his time with acting busy—instead of doing the most important things, the things that will generate sales.

- How should you follow up with and prioritize prospects?
- How can you avoid Danny's problem of shortchanging everyone when it comes to your time and attention and shortchanging yourself when it comes to closing sales?
- How can you organize your day to spend most of your time with prospects who are qualified and most likely to buy?

In this chapter, you will find out how to handle situations when there is a qualified prospect but a one-call close is impossible—or where it was in the selling process you lost that opportunity.

FOUR THINGS DANNY COULD BE DOING

Part of Danny's problem is that he doesn't yet have a day-in, day-out mastery of some of the keys to success we have already discussed. Just knowing about the best practices is not enough. You need to take action on them. Here's a quick recap of four habits that could help Danny do a better job of investing his most precious commodity—time.

1. **Walk in the door with everything you need to close the sale.** Danny is usually missing something or other, and he agrees to talk to one spouse when two should be present. Even if a one-call close is unusual in your industry, you should at least position yourself to close on the first call if the opportunity arises. That means scheduling appointments that include all the decision makers and making sure you have the samples, agreements and all other collateral you need in the event that the prospects do want to move forward.
2. **Schedule enough time.** Danny routinely runs short on time, which forces the dreaded "just email me the quotes" request. That's Danny's issue, not the prospect's, because he didn't ask for enough time. Allow the right amount of time for each appointment. Don't shortchange yourself.
3. **Know how the prospect will sell your stuff.** During those calls when he's meeting with a single spouse, Danny closes

the meeting by asking, "Do you have any questions?" When the prospect says, "No," Danny's out the door, eager to send the quote that night. But he's asking the wrong question. He needs to know exactly what's happening next and who's going to say what to whom. Figure out where you stand before you leave the appointment.

4. **Get a clear next step at the end of each appointment or call.** Danny's so busy that he's a little vague on the agreements about who will be connecting with whom, when and about what. He typically concludes his meeting by asking, "Can I call you back next week?" Even if all you do is set up a time for a call when both parties are home before you email a quote, you should make sure both sides agree on the specifics and are committed to them. Setting a mutually agreeable date and time on the calendar is far better than leaving with a vague next step, which is really no next step at all. Remember: No "think it overs." If there's resistance to that next step, it's your job to find out why.

"I DO ALL THAT ALREADY!"

Even if you do everything you just read about perfectly, there are going to be times when you need to follow up with a prospect after the initial meeting concludes. That means you will have to prioritize whom to contact and how. You will also need to figure out the most effective way to move prospects to the point where they close the sale themselves.

Most in-home salespeople don't understand follow up and prioritization. Management plays a big role here. Most managers tell their people to follow up with anyone who has a pulse and are frustrated with the lack of follow through that results from this instruction. Faced with this kind of leadership (or lack thereof), in-home salespeople tend to fall into a few familiar negative routines.

- They follow up diligently for "as long as it takes," even becoming a pest in situations where it is obvious the person is not going to buy.
- They ignore the manager and hardly ever follow up because they "can't find the time."
- They follow up but with a bad attitude because they think following up feels like begging. (The attitude here is, "If they want it, they will call me.")
- They follow up in exactly the same way with each prospect, no matter what happened during the discussion. For example, a salesperson has a "system" for following up where he always leaves one phone message after emailing the quote to "check in" and "answer any questions." The messages hardly ever produce return calls.

One problem with all of these patterns is that they do not allow the salesperson to prioritize and follow up in a way that keeps prospects who are most likely to buy moving towards a decision. Another problem—a big one—is that each of these approaches wastes the salesperson's most precious commodity—time.

REMEMBER: YOU ARE ON PAY TIME

As a sales professional, you must never forget that your time is your most valuable asset. If you were an attorney or a CPA, you would be aware of what client you should be billing for every phone call, discussion or email—almost for every thought. Sometimes, in the world of commissioned sales, we don't have the same approach. Consider some of the traps that can keep you busy but are not pay time. How much time does each activity below consume during the average work week?

- Going on a two-hour sales call where you spend most of your time discussing sports—but you run out of time before you get to the customer's problems and are asked to "send a quote."
- Failing to plan out your day and, as a result, spending unproductive time on the road.
- Setting appointments that do not happen.
- Playing phone tag and exchanging voicemails, but never actually connecting with prospects.
- Allowing service issues to expand in order to avoid making prospecting calls or calls with people who are expecting to hear from you.

And one last one that surprises people:

- Doing quotes!

Maybe you're wondering: "How can doing quotes not be pay time?"

Quotes are necessary, yes, but they should not be done during prime selling time—unless you are with the customer.

Some salespeople spend a lot of their prime appointment/prospecting time working on quotes. Often they then send those quotes out with no further conversation with the prospect. Ask them why they do that, and they'll say something like, "You can't close a sale without a quote, right?"

As we said earlier, by the time you do the quote, you should have a clear understanding of the pain. You should have discussed a price range or budget that is acceptable to the prospect, and you should understand the decision-making process. You should have a clear next step. If any one of those elements is missing, you are very likely spending too much time quoting business that never translates into commission dollars. That's not pay time!

If the prospect refuses to meet with you again in person and insists that you email the quote, guess what? That's a sign that you don't have a qualified prospect. It is always better to go back and deliver a quote in person to one qualified prospect than it is to email quotes to a dozen unqualified prospects and get no response.

Some companies decide to stop using the word "quote" altogether because it sounds too easy to email. You may decide to start saying instead, "We can put together a customized solution that will help you solve _____ [their main problem you uncovered]. Typically, we will come back out and go over that with both you and [name of spouse or partner] so we can answer any questions. Then, you can decide whether or not it makes sense to move forward with the project. When is a good time next week?"

STEPS FOR CLOSING

What about sales that genuinely take several calls to close? We've trained companies that required more than ten appointments or discussions before they could realistically expect to bring a deal to completion. Certainly, these are larger and more complex sales. But even in these circumstances, the salesperson must "close" for something at every appointment.

In the in-home sale, there may be many different decisions or commitments that the prospect has to make along the way toward the final sale. If you are in a multi-call process, all you have to do is identify the sequential decisions or commitments that a prospect has to make as you go.

Let's use an example. Suppose you sell large luxury projects that require many interactions before the first down payment is made. This is probably a much longer sales cycle than you would ever even contemplate. Even so, there is a sequence of multiple little "closes" that must be made in order to secure the big close—a signed contract. That list might look like this:

- Phone call
- In-person meeting with client
- Discussions with architect and client
- Preliminary budget discussion with architect and client
- Tour of previous projects completed by contractor
- Pre-construction evaluation, soil analysis and site readiness
- Permits and county approvals
- Initial construction documents
- Finalized construction documents
- Construction itself

Notice that every step is a decision by the prospect that involves some commitment or action on the prospect's part. Not only that—every step also involves an up-front contract at the beginning and the end of each interaction. By breaking down your sales process into smaller, incremental steps, you will see the small "closes" that must occur along the way to the big close.

THE PROSPECT YOU DON'T RE-CONTACT MATTERS AS MUCH AS THE ONE YOU DO

Not long ago, we worked with a client selling expensive home remodeling services. We had previously discussed with the sales management team their steps or "template," and we all agreed that the prospects truly worthy of follow up were those willing to tour previous projects. Management had statistical data to show that prospects who refused a tour had a low close rate. Those who agreed to take a tour had a much higher closing rate—roughly 75%.

One day, as we were training, a manager asked us how to close a client who refused to do a tour of previous projects. We explained that if a prospect wouldn't agree to do a free tour, the opportunity was, for all intents and purposes, done. No further sales activity was appropriate until the prospect agreed to do a free tour.

The sales team wasn't happy with our recommendation, even though there was strong evidence collected over several years that showed that a prospect unwilling to take this simple step was highly unlikely to become a customer. The salespeople didn't understand how their prospects made decisions. They thought it was a no-brainer for them to ask their prospects to take a day to tour past projects. However, while this company's prospects were what most would consider to be very wealthy, what they had only a little of was time. It was a major decision to use an entire day for a "free" tour.

Here was the approach we taught the salespeople to use to set an up-front contract at the beginning of the appointment:

"Jerry and Cindi, I appreciate you inviting me in again today. The purpose of our meeting is to further discuss how we might help you build your home. Since we last met, you may have thought of some additional questions for me, and I have some as well for you. At the end of our time we should know whether it makes sense to set up a tour of one of our completed properties. Or, if for some reason we don't think we should move forward, that is OK, too. Sound good?" [If the client's answer is "yes":] "Has anything changed since we last met?" [At this point, the salesperson could get back into questions, and focus on what's important to the client.]

Here is the approach we taught them to use at the end of the meeting when the couple expressed interest, but said they were busy and not sure when they could take the time to take the tour.

"Jerry and Cindi, I understand you're busy. Other couples like you, however, have found that by taking a tour of some of our other projects, they were able to visualize what might work for them and eliminate their concerns that building their dream house would be too time consuming or outside their budget. Is this something important enough to you to schedule next week?"

Typically the couple either committed to a time and date or, if they didn't, they proved that they were not qualified (even though they had plenty of money).

Three dynamics were at play here. First, the salespeople had no problem asking their prospects to make this decision about taking the tour (that was a good thing). They also shared a problem (pain) that others (third-party example) have felt and why it made sense for the prospects to take the tour. (Notice that they also set the stage for the decision to take the tour with a good up-front contract at the beginning of the appointment.) Second, the prospects revealed a whole lot about their intentions toward this company by agreeing to take a tour. Third, the prospects experienced a change in outlook by committing to take that concrete action. Once prospects agreed to take a day to do the tour, they changed how they felt about the relationship with the salesperson.

We've had extensive experience with companies that sell expensive or complex products. When we've asked them to outline the series of sequential sales steps or milestones, they initially react with disbelief. They say things like: "There are too many variables! We can't possibly predict what the steps are." Somehow, though, after 45 minutes, they are able to identify steps that aren't all that complex and are an excellent predictor of whether a prospect will eventually buy something.

Don't discount the importance of identifying all the key decision points or milestones prospects hit as they move through the process. If you are having trouble with this idea of multi-step closing, go back and look at your past clients. Examine what happened. A pattern will emerge. Your company may identify that there are only two or three steps, or there may be more than that. But whether you have a one-call close that takes place over a single discussion or a fifteen-step close that takes place over a series of weeks, you will find that there are multiple steps and every step can be identified.

> *All prospects are not created equal.*

PRIORITIZATION: ALL PROSPECTS ARE NOT CREATED EQUAL

So, in the end, who gets a quote?

To answer that, you need to create a system of priority that disqualifies people who are unlikely to buy. That means you don't do estimates for everyone. Have a clear idea about what needs to happen next that will help the people who are most likely to buy from you make the decision to do so. Find the low hanging fruit and take it. Don't work so hard!

When you do decide to provide a quote, how should you prioritize them? Here's a simple A, B, C ranking system you can use when you leave an appointment.

- **"A"**: All decision makers are present; you found pain (a problem) and they agreed the pain was important to fix within a certain time frame; you agreed on budget; and you have a clear next step that could be face-to-face, a time set to talk to go over the quote or a set time for a phone call to get a final decision.
- **"B"**: Prospect has pain, but there is some other key step missing. Maybe you didn't get any budget information or agreement; maybe he is getting another bid; maybe one of the decision makers was absent and you did not get a true "champion." Maybe the timeframe to make a decision is far in the future.
- **"C"**: Prospect is interested, but has some other issue. For whatever reason you were unable to move through the other stages of the sale with this person. Maybe the couple is checking around and might decide to do the work themselves. Be very careful not to do any unpaid consulting—

where you give them every part number and detail on how to do the work without you.

Some salespeople put a red (for not good); yellow (for maybe) and green (for go!) sticker on the outside of a folder or top of their note sheet so they can remember and prioritize their prospects. Whatever system you use, here are the key points to remember:

- Create a simple way to prioritize your prospects, especially if you are in an industry where you have many appointments day after day.
- Have a debrief or note sheet where you record: the clear next step you set; the pains you uncovered; and the budget and decision-making questions you may still need to discuss on the next call or appointment.
- Have a prioritized system for following up. Your system cannot be "just checking in." You must push to have a clear next step. If for some reason you are not able to set the date and time of that next discussion, you must provide a good reason (for them!) to get back in a conversation.

One more note about prioritization before we move on. Whenever you find yourself with an appointment that cancels or is delayed—hey, it happens!—make sure you use that time effectively. Pull out your cell phone and start calling those "A" prospects. They are your top priority. By the same token, you should call those "A" prospects first during those times you set aside to make your regular prospecting calls. They are your best time investments.

TO EMAIL OR NOT TO EMAIL?

Lots of people ask us whether they should use email as a follow-up tool. Yes, you should have creative email templates that you can use to follow up—but only so you can unstick opportunities.

Don't try to use email to close the deal. It doesn't work! Your job is to set up conversations that get you to a clear next step, and email can do that. The problem arises when you try to use email for an extended conversation.

Even on the phone, you can pick up by the tonality whether the prospect is more or less likely to buy. The same thing goes for voicemail. But leaving a "checking in" voicemail does not mean the prospect will take a next step. The same thing goes for the email messages you send. You must give people a reason to connect with you at a certain time, either voice-to-voice or face-to-face. Avoid phone and email tag.

The point is to have a conversation. Creative messages should make the prospect want to talk with you. Don't use email or voicemail to deliver a lengthy explanation of why to buy.

Here is an example of an effective follow-up email to a prospect, from salesperson Susan. Let's assume Susan sells for a siding company, and, for whatever reason, she did not manage to get a clear next step at the end of her appointment. Notice in the email below that her subject line is not "Checking in," or "Following up," or "Hope you are doing well." The subject is related to a problem she can solve. Are you beginning to see a pattern here? Interest in solving that problem is what's most likely to get the recipient to open the email.

SUBJECT: Eliminate painting

Juan,

When we met last week, you and Janie said you were considering siding for your home because:

- You were frustrated with the impact the winter had on your exterior paint and how it looked.
- Neither of you had the time to paint the house yourselves or find a reliable contractor year after year.
- You were concerned about the cost of keeping the home looking nice and may want to sell in a couple of years.

If these are still important, let's sit down again for about 30 minutes. I can go over the quote and the different options that may be important to you both. You can get all your questions answered and decide if it makes sense to move forward. If not, that is OK too.

I will call you at 9:00 Monday so we can set up an evening to meet.

Sincerely,

Susan Cunningham

(contact info)

While we're at it, here's an example of an effective follow-up voicemail message:

"Juan, Susan Cunningham with Sandler Siding. I have an idea [or question] that might be important. Call me at _____."

That's it! Not too wordy. Not too long. The object is to generate a return call so you can have a conversation. Of course, you must be ready to ask a key question or share an idea when the person calls.

You could also leave a message that relates back to his pain: "Juan, Susan Cunningham. You had a big concern about the installation. I have an idea. Call me at _____."

THE BOTTOM LINE

Sometimes it's easy to think that the job is to do as many quotes as possible, email those quotes and leave lots of messages, all in the hope that prospects will hunt us down to buy.

Instead, your job is to start conversations that generate decisions—small decisions at first, and bigger decisions as the sales process moves forward. That's the objective of effective follow through: to create more conversations that lead to a clear decision.

BOTTLENECKS AND SHORT SALES CYCLES

Most manufacturers know about bottlenecks. Those are the places in the manufacturing process that are slower than the rest. Bottlenecks constrain manufacturers' ability to make products. Rather than worry about the entire process, manufacturers focus on removing bottlenecks to increase capacity and decrease costs.

Selling is a process as well. Bottlenecks can plague salespeople and reduce their effectiveness. For example, consider follow-up calls. If a salesperson could close all his sales in one appointment rather than two, his sales capacity would double. Simple math, right? Yet this kind of math is not at all obvious to most sales teams. They think they should invest extra effort tracking down prospects hoping to get a sale.

As you've already learned, you can look more closely at your own process to identify the good prospects in order to focus your efforts on them. It's easier to make your sales process twice as efficient than to double the number of estimates you provide. Even if you don't have many leads, you can free yourself up to do more prospecting by shortening your sales cycle.

Sometimes bottlenecks are not obvious. For instance, many sales processes are stalled by the estimating process. Salespeople think they have to go back to the office and work up complex calculations. Designers or engineers think they have to create drawings or conduct an analysis. While these actions may not always be within the control of the salesperson, they can be bottlenecks in the selling process.

If the client says he wants to buy, make it easy for him to do so. Many salespeople choose the more time-consuming, deal-killing option of accepting the verbal agreement and then setting up another time so they can go back to the office, retrieve an agreement and then bring it back to the homeowner to sign. They are adding unnecessary steps to their own sales process—and losing sales. Use whatever technology that is available to obtain the formal agreement to allow the customer to buy now.

TIME KILLS DEALS

Occasionally we hear salespeople say, "I lost the deal for reasons out of my control." They explain that the homeowner got laid off, or someone got sick, or the competition came out with a new product.

It doesn't really matter. Time was under their control.

The longer their sales cycle, the greater the likelihood that these "uncontrollable" events will occur. That's today's world.

You must turn your time into money. The more efficient you

> **FOUR LEVELS OF PROSPECT COOPERATION**
> - *Level 4: Demands quote with no promise of further discussion, phone call or action.*
> - *Level 3: Agrees to review estimate on the phone; you send an email while you are both on the phone.*
> - *Level 2: Agrees to clear next step with a future meeting in person to decide on the estimate.*
> - *Level 1: Agrees to make a decision before the meeting is over.*
>
> *Of the four groups outlined above, which group do you think should win the lion's share of your time?*

are with your time, the more money you make. It's this feature that attracts many people into sales. You have control over your schedule, and your pay is a function of your success at consistently exerting that control.

Not all prospects will cooperate. Some will refuse any aspect of your up-front contract and the steps you outline for them. Some will refuse to cooperate with you even though it is in their best interests to do so. While this may be frustrating, you can still learn from the situation. Begin to notice, learn and rank the prospect's willingness to cooperate. This is a powerful tool for prioritization.

KEY TAKEAWAYS:

- Understand when you are on pay time and how to use it effectively.
- Prioritize your day and plan each call.
- Not all prospects are created equal; follow the system so you can easily know who is most likely to buy and act accordingly.
- Debrief after each call and note the clear next step in a multi-call sale.
- Use templates for email and phone calls that reinforce what was important to the prospect and generate action.

In the next chapter, you'll see how the Sandler Selling System works from start to finish—and how it can improve your results on your next appointment.

CHAPTER EIGHT

Putting It All Together

Now that you have a good understanding of how all the puzzle pieces fit together, you're probably wondering how it all plays out in an actual in-home selling appointment.

What you've gotten so far is a close-up of each step in the selling process. This chapter describes the flow of the selling process, from the initial lead intake to the in-home meeting itself. By following the system outlined below, you will be able to focus more on the customer—and spend less time trying to figure out how you are going to respond.

Remember: If you don't follow a consistent selling process, you default to the buyer's system. If that happens, you will never be sure where you are in the process, you will have a lot of "think it overs" to deal with and you will spend more time on follow up and "checking in" than you do putting money in the bank.

> *No winging it!*

THE FIRST IMPRESSION

Usually, the successful in-home selling process starts with a ringing phone answered by a professional and upbeat voice:

Inside Salesperson: "Thank you for calling Rapid Remodelers—how can I help you? "

Claire: "Uh, I was calling about getting a bid for replacing my countertops."

Inside Salesperson: "We're glad to hear that. What made you call us today?" [Remember to match tonality and pace of the caller.]

Claire: "I saw my neighbor's new countertops yesterday, and I want to get something similar. She said your company installed them, and they look great!"

Inside Salesperson: "We so appreciate referrals from our customers. Who is your neighbor?"

Claire: "Liza Dole. They redid their entire kitchen, but we just need some countertops."

Inside Salesperson: "Yes, we remember helping Liza. What is your name?"

Claire: "Claire Cool. I live in the Highlands area."

Inside Salesperson: "What did you like about her countertops?"

Claire: "She chose granite, and the color is gorgeous. It seems much easier to clean, too."

Inside Salesperson: "What type of countertops do you have now?"

Claire: "We have older Formica. It has some permanent stains and is not aging well."

Inside Salesperson: "What kinds of things caused the stains that won't come out?"

Claire: "Well, we have a wine stain and some burns from a hot pan—nothing seems to work on those."

Inside Salesperson: "I understand. Other customers call us because they are frustrated with their own countertops once they see some of the new ones available and want to get something easier to clean and that will improve the look of their home. Would you like us to bring some samples for you to see?"

Claire: "Sure!"

Inside Salesperson: "When would you be available to meet with one of our representatives?"

Claire: "Tuesday mornings work for me."

Inside Salesperson: "Was there someone else there at your home who will have an opinion about the countertops?"

Claire: "My husband, possibly."

Inside Salesperson: "If he could be there on Tuesday morning as well—"

Claire: "Yes, he can. He works from home."

Inside Salesperson: "Great! If you are able to choose some options that fit your budget, what did you want to do next?"

Claire: "What do you recommend?"

Inside Salesperson: "Typically you'd decide to invite some of our installers out to do a precision template."

Notice what happened here. The inside salesperson greeted the prospect professionally; asked questions to get her talking and find out what was important to her; and inquired in a professional way whether all decision makers would be present. Your industry may have additional questions that you need on your call intake template. Or, you may be in an industry where a few key questions and converting to an appointment are appropriate.

It is a good practice to follow up with a personalized email to confirm the appointment. In that email, you should offer a few bullets about why other customers have chosen your company and mention something about Claire and her particular pain to reinforce her decision to meet. Be sure to share this information with the salesperson who will be going out on the appointment.

To continue with this story, the salesperson David arrived a few minutes before the appointment time so he could conduct his pre-call planning. While he had been on hundreds of leads like this before, he had found that showing up five or ten minutes beforehand allows him to concentrate and get into "sell mode" and out of "talk mode." This also gives him plenty of time to prepare his questions and review the information he got from the inside salesperson. When appointment time rolled around, he knocked on the door.

David: "My name is David and I'm with Rapid Remodelers."

Claire: "Hello—you are right on time. Thank you for

coming over. Please come in. Let me get Joe and show you the kitchen."

Note: In general, you want to sit down with the customer before focusing on the area that needs to be replaced/repaired. You can get into trouble if you look at something too early because usually that means you won't talk to the customer again until you are quoting a price. Instead of accepting this invitation to see the area in question, ask to sit down. Then, give an up-front contract and ask some questions, so you can identify pain.

In this case, though, the kitchen area is where David wants to go to sit anyway. He looks briefly at the counters and asks if the three of them can sit down for a few minutes before he gets the samples so he can go over his up-front contract:

David: "How long are you going to be available today?"

Claire: "Well, they said it may take an hour. After that, Joe has a conference call and I have to leave."

David: "Good. I'll have some questions for you about what's most important with this project; you may have some questions for me about what we do and the different options for your countertops. At the end of our meeting today we should know whether we have something that might work for your home within your budget—if not, that is OK, too. If we do decide to move forward, you can decide if you would like a technician to do an exact measure for the cutting process. Sound good?"

David usually starts by asking more general questions like, "What don't you like about the countertops?" or "What seems to be the problem?" Then he either uses standard pain questions that apply to almost every homeowner or asks questions specific to this appointment that he prepared in advance during his pre-call planning.

David: "Tell me about what you don't like about the countertops you have now."

Claire: "They make our home look old, and they have stains that won't come out."

David: "When you say old, what do most homes in the area have?"

Joe: "Most people have changed to granite, stone or tile. We don't even like to have people over because it doesn't look good."

David: "Oh?"

Claire: "We avoid having people other than family or friends of the kids. We just think a new countertop would make things nicer."

David: "Give me an example of what you have tried to do to get the stains out."

Joe: "Everything. All kinds of cleaning products. We even tried a high-tech bleach that just made it worse. But, even if the counters were clean, they are still making our home dated."

David: "How long have you been thinking about changing out the countertops?"

Joe: "For a few years. But, other priorities came up. When we saw Liza's, it made us realize we needed to look into it."

David: "Besides seeing Ms. Dole's, have you looked at anything else?"

Claire: "No, not really. Just some stuff in magazines. I do know we like the material she has the best. What type of material did she get?"

David: "Quartz. Is there a reason you are asking?"

Claire: "Yes, I remember her saying that it's more heat resistant so we're less likely to get the burn marks, and there's no chance for bacteria to build up."

David: "If you don't get these replaced, what do you think will be the impact?"

Claire: "That would be very disappointing. It's been frustrating for the last two years. We have some events coming up when we'd like to have people over. We want to get it done as soon as possible."

Next David will ask about budget before getting samples for the prospect.

David: "So I make sure I respect your budget and only bring in samples that will work, would you share with me the range you want to stay within to fix your countertops?"

Claire and Joe discuss ranges based on the type of products. David agrees to bring a "good" and "better" sample like the Doles purchased, but sets the stage so there are no big budget surprises at the end. David thinks to himself that the budget will require him to use one slab, but resists the temptation to go into a long explanation about trying to match slabs.

David gets the samples. While Claire and Joe are looking at them, he measures the countertops and keeps engaged, making sure they talk 70% and he talks 30%. Meanwhile, Claire finds the perfect sample.

Claire: "I want it to look exactly like this!"

David: "Redwood Sparkle is a great choice." [David resists the temptation to discuss the colors and pattern variation in quartz.] "When you say you want it to look exactly like this, what do you mean?"

Claire: "The colors and the metallic flake match the kitchen perfectly."

David: "Did you expect the pattern to be identical as well?"

Claire: "No, Liza already explained there might be some variation in the pattern."

Liza did a great job paving the way. After David has the dimensions and realizes the work can be done with one slab, he helps them select a couple of options for the edging. He shares only information important to them (instead of going through every feature of the product) and then makes sure he asks them how the overall plan would work for them.

He sits back down at the table while writing up the proposal. He then reviews the pain (getting them to talk); reviews their budget and how their chosen options fit; gets agreement; discusses that they said they would both make the decision today if it made sense; and asks his closing question.

David: "Based on this solution, what would you like to do?" [This is the most powerful closing line when you have done everything right!]

Claire: "Place the order!"

After David gets the contract, payment terms, detailed measure and installation date set up, he uses the Post-Sell Step to prevent buyer's remorse:

David: "Can we look at that pattern one last time? Are you sure it's the colors and not the exact pattern that you like?"

Claire: "We know that the pattern may vary, and that will be fine. As long as these same colors come out in the slab, I know we are going to love it."

David: "We are looking forward to getting the new countertops set up for you."

Note: This works for them to reinforce their decision and can be very important if you are unseating a current or prospective other vendor. In that case, you might say: "How will you handle letting ABC vendor know that you have made a decision to go with this solution?" Be quiet; let them reinforce why they selected you and your solution.

Now David can also ask for introductions/referrals.

David: "Have you spoken to any of your other neighbors besides Liza? Who else do you know in the neighborhood who, like you, might be frustrated with the older type of countertops and would like to update their home for resale or have it to look more modern?"

David wraps up the meeting, establishes the next step with Claire and Joe and says goodbye. He spends a few minutes in his car making notes on his debrief: what went well; where he could improve; and what additional information might he need for the installation/follow up. And he's had a very good day.

MULTI-STEP SALES EXAMPLE

Suppose Claire and Joe had decided that, in addition to the quartz countertops, the cabinets are dated and need replacing and the floor should be replaced along with the backsplash and a fresh paint job. Suppose David did such a great job finding pain that the couple decided they wanted their entire kitchen to look brand new!

This would result in a multiple-call sell. So, what changes from the previous example?

Let's start at the beginning. If David had known going in that it would be a bigger project, his up-front contract might have been different. Here is an example:

> **David:** "You said you had a couple of hours today to discuss your kitchen remodeling. Is that still good?" [It is.] "Great. I'll ask you some questions about your vision and what you would like to change; I'll answer your questions about what we offer and how we have helped other couples update their homes. At the end of our meeting today, we should know whether it makes sense to move forward with a design. If not, that is OK as well. How does that sound?"

The rest of the steps are similar: David starts by finding pain; he always keeps the customers talking about what is important to them. He focuses on the "why" and the impact of getting their kitchen remodeled. Budget is critical, of course, and may need to be discussed at each appointment as the project goes along. Decision making is also a key issue, since David may not be dealing with all decision makers at each appointment. The key thing to remember in this type of sale is you always need a clear next step.

A vague next step is:

Claire: "David, these samples look good. Let us look at these for a couple of weeks and then give us a call."

That sounds pretty good to most salespeople. Look how David responds, though.

David: "I'm glad to hear that you think you will find some good options with those samples. Typically, customers like to set a time for a follow up after comparing samples. I know I am out in the field, and you are both busy as well. Let's set a date to spend an hour, go over the samples that might work and decide whether we price those on the master plan and go on to the next phase or whether we need some different options. Either way is OK. At least we are moving to make sure you get the house looking less dated." [Note David reinforces their pain.] "What time works for you both?"

Claire: "Friday at 3:00 P.M. How long will we need?"

David: "Usually an hour. Is there a reason you are asking?"

Joe: "Yes, we need to attend a function at church at 4:30 P.M. that Friday."

So, David does a post-sell on the appointment:

David: "Do you think Friday traffic might be worse and you both might not have enough time to get home or to the church later?"

Joe: "No, the church is close to us. But thanks for asking."

David: "Will there be enough time to finalize your choices and options?"

Claire: "Actually, I'm going to pick the options tomorrow and leave them on the dinner table so Joe can look at them before Friday. I don't want either one of us deciding at the last minute."

David: "That's perfect. So all we will do is go through the choices, select which ones to add to the master plan and then set an appointment at our design offices for one final review and approval."

Notice how David is not only setting the next appointment, he is outlining what decision should be made.

On a multiple meeting sale like a larger remodel, you may be closing for a clear next step to:

- Review and select samples/designs.
- Go see another project/go to a design center.
- Meet with other key players (i.e., architect, project manager).
- Discuss interim proposals/pricing.
- Decide on implementation schedule.

The examples depicted above show David following the Sandler Selling System. He doesn't have to guess or rely on "hopium" to determine whether or not he is moving forward in the sales process with the prospects. He knows! The homeowners are likely to see him less as a salesperson and more as a consultant. Homeowners like Claire and Joe are much more likely to buy from David again later and refer David to their neighbor. David feels better about his time management and role as a problem solver and a valued consultant.

SUMMARY: ANATOMY OF A GREAT IN-HOME SALES CALL

First Impressions Matter

- On the initial phone call, use a professional and welcoming tone.
- First question: "What made you call today?" Look for pain insights and referral sources.
- Continue to ask questions; the more customers talk, the more engaged they are and the less likely they are to call a competitor.
- Be able to share a little about why other homeowners have selected your company.
- Transition to an appointment with an up-front contract about next steps.
- Be sure to obtain a good way to confirm the appointment (phone/email).

In-Home Sales Appointment

- Review lead intake form.
- Use pre-call planning.
- Arrive at the appointment on time.
- Use matching and mirroring, and note any predominant communication style.

Set the Stage for Success: Up-Front Contract

- State an up-front contract before you look at the home in detail. Sit down with the client.
- Include time, purpose, both agendas, and possible outcomes.

Example: "Mrs. Smith, do we still have about an hour today to [purpose]? Great. I'll ask you some questions about what you are looking for; you probably have some questions for me about why other customers in the area have selected [company name]. At the end of the call, we should know whether there is any reason to move forward; and if not, that is OK. If we do decide to move forward, we can talk about the next steps to get your [product or service] set up. How does that sound?"

- Once the homeowners have agreed with your up-front contract, ask specific questions to find pain or share examples of pains that other customers have had to determine if any of them apply to these prospects.

Example: "Let me share a few of the key reasons customers have come to us:

- "Some are frustrated because they have had a prior experience with an in-home repair, and there were problems throughout the process.

- "Other customers are overwhelmed with all that needs to be done while getting their home ready for sale, and they want a professional team to handle these problems.

- "Customers have also told us they are concerned about getting the best value while making sure the quality and warranties are what they need.

- "Which if any of these are important to you?"

Get the Customer to Talk 70% of the Time

- Ask pain questions while discussing the project. Do not show your samples or present yet. Instead, ask, "Tell me

about..." "How long..." "What have you tried..." "How did that work..." "What is the impact if you do not act by..." "Is it important to fix..." etc.
- Use questioning techniques to fully understand the pain (customer talks 70%; you talk 30%). Note: You may hear about some aspects of the pain while sitting with the customer or as you review the area of opportunity. However, do not start working on a solution before engaging the prospect's pain fully.
- Ask about budget: share, use third-party stories, round numbers, and bracket.
- Ask about the decision-making process and who needs to be involved/consulted. Discuss your company's process and the steps entailed.
- Cover timing and criteria. When does the prospect want to complete the project, start the project, and pick a contractor?

Fulfillment

- Craft a solution based on pain and the prospect's budget and compatible with the decision-making process you have discussed previously—not a laundry list of every feature you offer.
- Keep the customer engaged. Don't be the only one talking, but ask, "How will this solve your ____ problem?"
- If you are not speaking to the only decision maker, ask what the other (typically a spouse) will need to see. Make note of those things during the fulfillment stage so you can deliver the information the inside coach needs to champion the project.

- Manage the process to stay within budget or have a discussion about it before the end of the presentation. Do not make false promises on low prices at the beginning—this will result in a more satisfied client at the end.
- If you have done a good job, you can let the customer close the sale. "Do you think this solution will meet your needs? What do you see as the next step?"
- If dealing with a inside coach, ask, "Based on what you have seen, are you going to recommend that we move forward?" If "yes," ask, "What about the solution do you think will help you the most?"
- If you didn't close the sale on this call, get a clear next step. Do not agree to "check back in a few weeks."

Example: "Bob, I know you are busy, and I am out in the field handling appointments. Other customers typically like to set a specific time to talk [or meet] and go over the quote. There are some different options, and most people have a few questions that come up after I leave. As I mentioned when I came in, if [our company] is not the right solution, it is OK to tell me 'no.' This way, I can answer your questions and you can decide on the next step without us playing phone tag and taking more time. How does Wednesday evening next week at 6:00 sound?"

- If possible:
  - Single-call close is the best.
  - Next best: Have a reason and make an appointment to get back in front of all decision makers.
  - Next best: Have a set time for a phone call. You can email after the call starts (with a "what's in it for them"

approach and including the *no* as an option to cement credibility).
- Next best: Send an email with a time/date request to review quote.
- If you must: Send an email with clear bullets on the prospect's pain and your solution and a time/date for a follow-up call.
- Avoid at all costs: Blindly sending a quote with "call me with any questions."

Close the Sale

- Close the sale and ask about introductions (can also ask even if you don't close the sale).
- Use the Post-Sell Step to make sure the prospect doesn't have buyer's remorse, especially if another vendor has been or will be contacted.
- Debrief privately. Review what you did well, where you could improve, next steps and critical information.

THE ROAD FROM HERE

This book has given you a road map for sales and key areas where sales leaders should focus to exceed sales goals for their company.

Some clients have told us they were initially worried about implementing a new process or structure. They thought sales might dip if they asked their people (and themselves) to do something different.

What you will find—what our clients have found—is that implementing any part of the Sandler concepts can create incremental positive change. Commit to a few ideas in this book and practice them consistently, and you will start to see improvement. You do not need to master every single concept in this book before you begin implementation and improve your sales performance.

A WORD OF WARNING TO SALES MANAGERS AND BUSINESS OWNERS

Now that you have read the book, you probably will do one of two things:

1. Put the book away, maybe thinking about implementing one or two ideas.

~or~

2. Take control of the selling process by learning more and improving your sales results.

We understand the in-home selling market and the unique challenges and opportunities you face in the home. We also recognize the manager's ability to lead the sales team is crucial. Resist the temptation to hand this book to your staff with instructions like, "Fred, why don't you read this book and give it a try?" In order to get salespeople to change habits, management must be supportive and willing to allow a few stumbles along the path of improvement.

The manager must also assist the salesperson in the proper execution of many of these techniques and strategies. For instance, setting an up-front contract on the phone prior to the appointment will almost certainly require assistance from the inside team or gentle reminders to the salesperson. The manager should review the use of the selling system after every call to make it a habit. Asking his salespeople about the questions they asked and placing less emphasis on what they said or left behind is another. The manager must stop asking questions like, "So do you think the prospect will buy?" Instead, start having tactical discussions about the information and commitments the salesperson obtained in the sales meeting (example: ask about pain, budget, decision making, and clear next steps).

Some of the Sandler concepts may at first appear to be counterintuitive. Disqualifying a prospect, being a dummy on purpose, not talking features and benefits and holding off on a presentation are just a handful of examples where the sales manager or owner must support the salesperson in spite of conventional wisdom or "the way we've always done it." For managers to become leaders, they must embrace these same skills. A boss says, "Go," but a leader says, "Let's go!" To maximize the impact of this book on your sales organization, we strongly suggest managers roll up their sleeves and get involved in the change process.

We are here to help you continue to develop in both sales and sales management. You are invited to attend one of our local Sandler training classes at no charge to see how we have helped other businesses and how we can help you achieve your goals. Contrary to popular belief, great salespeople are not born—they have learned to sell. The Sandler Selling System is a great way to learn.

We hope that this book has helped you and your team along that path. Stay in touch! Go to www.sandler.com/sellingtohomeowners for more information on finding a local class and to get the latest updates and advice.

Look for these other books
on shop.sandler.com:

Prospect the Sandler Way

Transforming Leaders the Sandler Way

Selling Professional Services the Sandler Way

Accountability the Sandler Way

Selling Technology the Sandler Way

LinkedIn the Sandler Way

Bootstrap Selling the Sandler Way

Customer Service the Sandler Way

CONGRATULATIONS!

Selling to Homeowners the Sandler Way
includes a complimentary seminar!

Take this opportunity to personally experience the non-traditional sales training and reinforcement coaching that has been recognized internationally for decades.

Companies in the Fortune 1000 as well as thousands of small- to medium-sized businesses choose Sandler for sales, leadership, management, and a wealth of other skill-building programs. Now, it's your turn, and it's free!

You'll learn the latest practical, tactical, feet-in-the-street sales methods directly from your neighborhood Sandler trainers! They're knowledgeable, friendly and informed about your local selling environment.

Here's how you redeem YOUR FREE SEMINAR invitation.

1. Go to www.Sandler.com and click on Find Training Location (top blue bar).
2. Select your location.
3. Review the list of all the Sandler trainers in your area.
4. Call your local Sandler trainer, mention *Selling to Homeowners the Sandler Way* and reserve your place at the next seminar!